REMEMBERING
PAULE

A Photo Memoir of Her Richmond Years

Daryl Cumber Dance

REMEMBERING Paule

A Photo Memoir of Her Richmond Years

ISBN 978-1-962729-00-0

Published in the United States of America by Inspire, an Adducent nonfiction imprint.

Adducent, Inc.

Jacksonville, Florida

AdducentCreative.com

CONTENTS

ADVANCE PRAISE

"There are many ways and reasons to love someone: kindness; thoughtfulness; warmth; patience; always being there for you. When my son was born Paule Marshall was the first person to visit me and bring congratulations and a present. I always loved her for that. When you read *REMEMBERING Paule* by Daryl Dance you will discover your own reasons for loving Daryl and Paule. A glass of wine, a quilt over your feet and a wonderful book. Who could ask for more?"

—Nikki Giovanni, Poet

"I am so grateful for Daryl Cumber Dance's stunning testament to her friendship with Paule Marshall. She held the treasured memories of Paule in her heart and mind until she could do justice to the specialness of their friendship. *REMEMBERING Paule is* magnificently worth the wait!"

—Joanne Veal Gabbin, Founder of the Wintergreen Women Writers Collective

"Daryl Cumber Dance has written an exquisite, meticulous and warmhearted paean to her dear friend, colleague, and fellow traveler, the novelist Paule Marshall. Dance regales the reader with countless scholarly activities and social events involving colleagues and friends literally across the globe from Richmond to Paris. *REMEMBERING Paule* is a delight, and it is also a powerful testament to the indispensable value of a lasting friendship."

—Alvin Schexnider, Academician, Genealogist

"What a gift it is to be given such a clear window into the extraordinary friendship of these two phenomenal Black women writers! *REMEMBERING Paule* captures the dazzling and the quotidian moments, both anchored in indubitable fact and delightful photographs. Paule Marshall lives on—vibrantly, vividly—in Daryl Cumber Dance's detailed and precious memories."

—Lauren K. Alleyne, Executive Director, Furious Flower Poetry Center

"To read *REMEMBERING Paule* by Daryl Cumber Dance is to understand how the brilliant writer Paule Marshall—a Brooklyn native of Barbadian heritage —could be lured to join Dance in the English department at Virginia Commonwealth University. At first unnerved by the Confederate statues on Richmond's Monument Avenue, Marshall, author of the seminal 1959 novel *Brown Girl, Brownstones,* formed an unlikely bond with her adopted city. Dance, her supportive colleague, tour guide and friend, renders in painstaking detail a heartfelt tribute to Marshall, who died in 2019."

—Michael Paul Williams, Pulitzer Prize-Winning Journalist

DEDICATION

To my grands, Yoseph and Veronica,

As young adults, you have barely begun evolving the countless treasured memories that will delight you and your family through the years. Treasure, hold on to, and pass on the special memories.

Remember:

"Memory is the treasure house of the mind wherein the monuments thereof are kept and preserved." —Thomas Fuller

ACKNOWLEDGMENTS

This book could not have been possible without the quick responses of Alvin Schexnider, Quincy Moore, Esther Vassar, Trudier Harris, Mary DePillars, Burney Hollis, Joanne Gabbin, Opal Moore, and other friends and colleagues who responded to my frantic SOS when I sought pictures and when I needed some checks on my memory of our dear friend Paule Marshall.

Profound thanks are always due to my Wintergreen sisters, who, for thirty-six years, have been encouraging and inspiring me in every writing project I have undertaken.

As she has through the years, Marcia Whitehead of UR's Boatwright Library provided critical guidance and research information. As always, I am grateful for the support of the numerous computer technicians at the Help Desk at the University of Richmond, especially Orlando Stevens and Christina Sheppherson. Thanks, too, to Melissa Foster and her staff in UR's Technology Learning Center, who assisted me with the preparation of some of the visuals appearing here.

Special thanks are due to members of my family who **always** support my projects in ways too numerous to detail, especially Allen Cumber Dance, Warren Carlton Dance, Jr., Tadelech Edjigu Dance, and Daryl Lynn Dance.

I wish I could individually thank everyone who shared a picture with me that I have included here, but numerous pictures sent to me over many years are a part of the often-anonymous collection of pictures from which I drew for this work.

I am grateful to Dennis Lowery and his company Adducent's expertise and patience in working with me to bring this photo memoir to fruition.

INTRODUCTION

Literary friendships are themselves legend—often as fascinating and as melodramatic as the literary productions of the writers: Christ and John, Johnson and Boswell, Wordsworth and Coleridge, Byron and Shelley, Hawthorne and Melville, Fitzgerald and Hemingway, Hughes and Bontemps, Hughes and Hurston, Wright and Baldwin, King and Abernathy, Morrison and Bambara, Ginsburg and Totenberg. These friends often inspired, supported, informed, guided, collaborated, protected, advised, traveled, worked, partied, drank and dined together. But oftentimes several of these literary friends also conflicted, disagreed, envied, quarreled, attacked, abused, threatened, renounced, and even sued each other. Some of these relationships were long-standing, while others were relatively brief or sporadic. All these friendships were critical to the subjects themselves, to literary history, and to students and scholars of their works. Most of these relationships helped to change the course of literature, indeed to spark new movements.

REMEMBERING Paule is the compelling story of two such friends, novelist Paule Marshall and folklorist and literary critic Daryl Cumber Dance, both committed truth-tellers, teachers, cultural critics, writers, and activists who wielded their pens to revolutionize their literary world. Marshall is often hailed as the matriarch of the Black Women's Literary Renaissance. Morrison and Walker, who have often been acclaimed that honor, have both insisted that the distinction is due to Marshall. Marshall, herself, often acknowledges the earlier work of Brooks. All these women are notable trailblazers, but there is no doubt that Marshall's *Brown Girl, Brownstones* signaled a new day in African Diasporic women's writing. Daryl Dance has been dubbed "the Dean of American folklore" for her work in African American and Jamaican folklore. In Japan, she was greeted and celebrated by professors and scholars for providing them their "Bible," rare resources for the study of Caribbean literature. In their 2022 *Black Facts*, Tim and Deb Smith celebrate Dance as one of the four "Original Ladies of Black Comedy."

Following the death of Marshall, Dance details their thirty-five-year friendship, a congenial relationship lacking all of the drama, melodrama, and tragedy of a number of other literary friendships, but notable for their years of amiably working, traveling, lecturing, walking, dining, drinking, laughing, talking, and sharing together. Dance presents that friendship in what Alvin Schexnider has labeled "an exquisite, meticulous and warmhearted paean to her dear friend." Lauren K. Alleyne declares, "Paule Marshall lives on—vibrantly, vividly—in Daryl Cumber Dance's detailed and precious memories."

FOREWORD

When last I talked with Paule Marshall, my brilliant and eloquent friend—the foremost among those writers who issued in the Black Women's Renaissance—she was struggling under that cloud that was enveloping so many of my cohorts–that slowly descending veil that dimmed faces, confused details, and sometimes effaced memories. This conversation, unlike our innumerable enthusiastic exchanges through the years, was awkward and halting. It was clear that she was reluctant to continue, both frustrated and embarrassed by unstable memories that ranged from sharp and penetrating to vague, confused, disoriented, lost.

Immediately upon Paule's passing, some years later, on August 12, 2019, our mutual friend, Joanne Gabbin, asked me to provide a tribute to her. I wrote back on August 28:

> I'm so sorry that I haven't been able to write anything about Paule.... Paule was too special to me to try to rush something. At some point I'll give her the time she deserves for a thoughtful recollection.

Joanne understood and answered on August 28, 2019:

> Please don't worry about it. When it is time, you will give her a fitting tribute. What is important is that you were always a special friend to her. You respected her and her work, and she knew it.
>
> Love,
>
> Joanne

Ironically, about two-and-one-half years later, as that same ominous cloud occasionally threatens me, I suddenly awakened at 6:04 a.m., March 2, 2022, with vivid recollections of our friendship zooming through my mind like flashing pictures from a breaking news story.

I rushed to the computer and started writing.

--Daryl Cumber Dance

MEETING PAULE MARSHALL

Though I had long been an ardent fan of Paule Marshall's writing, I met the famed novelist face to face for the first time in The Hyatt Regency Hotel in New Orleans at the forty-first convention of the College Language Association (hereafter, CLA), sponsored by Xavier University in 1981. The theme of the conference was "The Plantation-America Culture Sphere: Caribbean and Southern Literatures." On Thursday, April 23, 1981, I presented a paper in the first session, "Three Journeys: Discussions with Caribbean Writers about the Quest for Identity." (The three journeys took them from their home nation to the colonizer's nation and then to Africa.) I did not treat Paule in my paper; however, as I look back, I view my subject as somewhat prophetic since throughout Paule's oeuvre, she was dedicated to the quest of bringing together Africans from Africa, the Caribbean, and the United States and discovering identity and home through closing the circle and achieving unity. In a later unpublished paper, "The Circle Be Unbroken," I returned to this theme, focusing on Marshall's Avey entering the circle at The Big Drum Ceremony and thereby becoming "centered... restored to her proper axis" (*Praisesong for the Widow* 254).

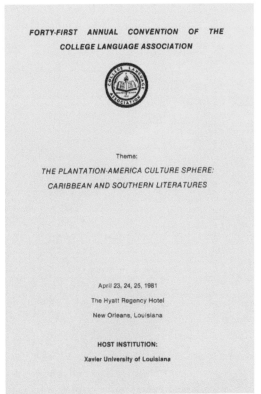

On Friday, April 24, Paule was the featured speaker at the CLA Banquet. Excited to see and hear her, I rushed to claim a front-row center seat at the event. Afterwards, I looked on from a distance as all the CLA nobility congratulated and chatted with her. As the crowd disbursed, I cautiously approached her, probably babbling about my enthusiasm for her work, possibly adding a hundredth congratulation for her presentation, maybe simply offering commiseration for all the lionizing to which she was being subjected. All I clearly remember is that we started a chat that lasted until the banquet hall was cleared, and then we moved on to the hotel bar, where we amiably and enthusiastically talked about everything from CLA to New York, to Richmond, to Barbados, to family and friends. Paule ordered a kir after first ascertaining that the bartender knew just how to prepare it to her liking. I don't recall what I had—possibly a glass of wine, a virgin pina colada, maybe just tonic and lime. We talked until the bar closed, by which time we had become friends, confidants, and partners with a mission. I recall that I promised to send her information about a few Caribbean writers and that we were to talk further about the possibility of her visiting Virginia Commonwealth University (hereafter, VCU).

We exchanged contact information and promised to keep in touch.

INVITING PAULE TO VIRGINIA COMMONWEALTH UNIVERSITY

My Chi[1] always prepares the way for critical journeys in my life, and certainly, it was her intercession that led the State of Virginia to, shortly after my meeting with Paule, allot an impressive sum of money to establish a Visiting Scholars Program to attract major Black scholars to the faculty of our state schools.[2] I forthwith initiated a series of correspondences in an effort to bring at least one outstanding Black writer to VCU. Indeed, since I was the only Black professor in the English Department, it wasn't beyond my admittedly wild imagination that we might hire **two** Black writers. On October 3, 1983, I wrote to Elske v.P. Smith, The Dean of the School of Arts and Sciences, asking her to consider nominating Edward Brathwaite, Toni Cade Bambara, Paule Marshall, and Derek Walcott, including brief but laudatory overviews of their extraordinary accomplishments. She asked me to contact them about the position, but in a letter the next day, I expressed my desire to wait to contact any one of these established writers until I was convinced that VCU would follow through. After further consultation with Dean Smith, Dorothy Scura (the Director of Graduate Studies and soon-to-be Chairman of the English Department), and the Creative Writing Faculty, I contacted Paule Marshall, ascertained her willingness to consider a two-year appointment at VCU, and requested a resume, which she sent and which I enthusiastically and promptly circulated. On November 28, 1983, the Dean wrote to Wayne Hall, Provost and Vice President, "I enclose a memorandum from Dr. Daryl Dance with a proposal that we request that Paule Marshall be nominated for the Commonwealth Visiting Professorship Program... Bringing Ms. Marshall would... give a real boost to the MA in Creative Writing Program." Later that day, after I had provided further information, she wrote another enthusiastic letter to Provost Hall, declaring, "I don't think we can find a more prominent candidate than Ms. Marshall," quoting directly the qualifications that I had provided her in my letter earlier that same day. With all parties enthusiastic about having Paule join us, I communicated with her regarding an appointment. I then passed on to the Dean her desire, as expressed in her letter to me of November 30, 1983, to accept a position that would allow her to teach two courses in the fall of '84 and '85, with no teaching assignments in the spring. Paule concluded her letter to me, "Again, thank you for submitting my name, and I look forward to hearing from you soon" (11/30/83). The Dean wrote to her, offering an appointment that incorporated all of Paule's concerns, and assured her that help would be provided in finding furnished housing. Paule's salary the first year was $25,000.00 plus benefits and a $10,000 allocation "for travel, secretarial support and other related expenses" (letter from Dean Smith, January 18, 1984).

And thus, Paule Marshall, after teaching during the spring semester of 1984 at the University of California at Berkeley, joined the faculty at VCU in September 1984, where she remained until 1994 when she retired as Emerita Professor and then moved on to New York University (NYU), where she held the Helen Gould Sheppard Chair of Literature and Culture for thirteen years.

In her last book, *Triangular Road: A Memoir* (2009), Paule wrote that she arrived in Richmond "Mid-August 1983, [with classes] scheduled to begin... the second week in September" (51). The fact is that she arrived in August 1984. She and a friend had driven from California in what I believe was Paule's first car. A typical New Yorker, Paule had not learned to drive until late in life, and I don't think she ever liked driving. During the years I knew her here in Richmond, other friends and I usually did the driving when we went anywhere with Paule. We were all eager to provide her whatever services we could, and providing her

---

[1] In Igbo Cosmology the Chi is one's guardian angel, perhaps an ancestral spirit.
[2] Nikki Giovanni, Ellis Marsalis, Maryse Condé, Rita Dove, Sherley Anne Williams, Albert Murray, Alexander Gabbin, and Joanne Gabbin were among those invited to Virginia universities through this program.

transportation was usually the most important service to her. The public transportation that she was accustomed to in larger cities wasn't readily available here: no subways, no visible taxis, only buses with limited areas and untrustworthy schedules. I don't think I ever rode in Paule's car. I don't even remember what it was or what it looked like. I think it was a small car, but the few times she drove it to my house, I didn't really see it—she usually parked on the side of my house, not visible to either of the entrances to my house at which I received her. (On October 14, 2023, at an event for Nikki Giovanni, a mutual friend told me Paule's car was a Volkswagen.)

Paule and her friend stayed at my house that first night, sleeping in our guest room and in our daughter's first bedroom—later, our grandbabies' room.

The next day, I took Paule for her first look at VCU. I don't recall her visible reaction to or commentary about the campus. Located in the historic Fan District, VCU was a truly urban university with considerable traffic, its Monroe Park Campus encompassing about twenty-three blocks of unremarkable three-story buildings housing faculty offices and classrooms (a bookstore in the basement of one of them [The Hibbs Building, which housed the English Department]), a few stately houses (then converted into executive offices, departments, and programs), and a library, with a few private houses, restaurants, and businesses (including one movie theater) sprinkled in between. The only buildings with any notable design were The Center of the Arts Building, the then-recently built Student Center, and the Business Building (this latter with **four** floors). There were a couple of "high-rise" student dorms, one eighteen floors high. The campus was mostly brick and stone, with a few buildings having a tiny plot of grass and

THE CENTER OF THE ARTS BUILDING

some rare flowers. There was an occasional parking lot. The Monroe Park Campus encompassed parts of Grace, Franklin, Park, Floyd, and Main Streets. The Eastern part of the campus extended to Monroe Park, The Mosque (Richmond's largest theater at the time), and The Cathedral of the Sacred Heart; and the Western part of the campus extended to Ryland Street. There was no football field, no baseball field, no tennis courts, no lake, and no fountain on the then-Monroe Park Campus. There were very few trees.

I did not take Paule to the Medical campus, two miles away. It was even more urban, also mostly brick and stone, but with taller buildings and heavier traffic. Almost no trees.

Remarkable growth would occur on the Monroe Park Campus during ensuing years. Park Avenue in front of Hibbs was closed to traffic, and that section was landscaped, creating something more of the campus ambiance found at most Virginia colleges, including some grass and trees.

THE INSTITUTE FOR CONTEMPORARY ART
PHOTO BY WARREN C. DANCE, JR

Then later, there was the expansion of the Cabell Library, and the building of a large Barnes and Noble Campus Book Store, a few parking decks, some more attractive student apartments, The Shafer Court Dining Center, The College of Engineering, The Siegel Center, The VCU Fine Arts Building (renamed The Murry N. DePillars Building in 2021), and The Thalhimer Tennis Center. The Institute for Contemporary Art, VCU's truly eye-stopping building, did not open until 2018, and it is likely that Paule never saw it.

I expect that this building would have elicited a resounding vote of approval from her.

As I write this in 2023, the expansion of the Monroe Park Campus continues—past Lombardy on the West, past Belvedere on the East, past Marshall on the North, and past Cumberland on the South. The many branches of the University reach far beyond the school that Paule knew. There is even one VCU research facility in Charles City (a rural county on the James, about thirty miles from Richmond).

On her first visit to VCU, I walked with Paule through The Hibbs Building so she could see her office and meet our Dean and other colleagues. Everything and everyone was new to Paule. The only VCU colleague that she had met before was Art Historian Regenia Perry. The next year, in September 1985, Quincy Moore, whom she had met in Iowa, would join us as Executive Director of VCU's Academic Success Center.

Paule stayed with my family for a few nights until we helped her settle into her furnished apartment in The Chesterfield (just one block from her VCU office).

Regenia Perry and I got together a few small items to tide her over as she set up her apartment.

Paule remained at The Chesterfield until she found a condo at 503 S. Davis Avenue, #6, one with a view of Swan Lake in Byrd Park, with its wonderful walking trails. She loved the view and the location—within walking distance of VCU, Carytown, and other areas of The Fan. The Fan District, the most artsy community in Richmond, boasts grand mansions, charming coffee shops, popular restaurants, and lively entertainment. Paule was a speed walker and would often, if it were still light, walk to the restaurants or the facilities we were attending for lectures, concerts, etc. Then I would take her home afterwards. Of course, I would pick her up if time, distance, and/or weather dictated. She never requested a ride, but I would always offer. I was the driver whenever we went anywhere together. She was always waiting at her door or on the street at—and usually before—the appointed time.

THE CHESTERFIELD

THE HIBBS BUILDING

Elated to have Paule on our faculty, I started working with my Chair and Dean to have her offered a permanent position at VCU. On July 10, 1985, I wrote a letter enthusiastically recommending that she be offered tenure as a full professor. When Dorothy Scura—then our chair—completed her final letter of recommendation, she wrote to ask me if I wanted to read it and concluded, "I appreciate your cooperation and help with this matter" (July 10, 1985). She almost immediately wrote to tell me that the Dean and Provost Charles Ruch were recommending the appointment to the President.

Paule and I had offices on the third floor of The Hibbs Building at VCU.

We were frequently together at University and Department events, including this May 1991 Commencement, where we are pictured with Quincy Moore.

Oddly enough, as I was writing this last paragraph on June 13, 2022, another one of those rare but related events occurred that I often attribute to my Chi. Quincy Moore texted me," You were the first black person I met at Virginia Commonwealth University with her own bathroom and her office."

Another memory sparked!

My first office at VCU, and the one I was in when Paule arrived, was in a high-traffic area, just across from the elevators and just around the corner from the main department office. Anyone going to other offices passed by my office. There was a steady din of noise from conversations of students waiting in the hallways or conversing with neighboring professors, and at least twice a week, there was a loud alarm from a stuck elevator almost directly across from me.

Then, out of the blue—and this too was probably the work of my Chi—or perhaps offers I was receiving from other universities—I was

PHOTO COMPLIMENTS OF QUINCY MOORE

proffered this special office, all by itself at the very end of the hall. No one ever passed by or gathered outside this office. It was really a suite with additional space for my many bookshelves, file cabinets, desks, and chairs—even a fridge. **And** it had a bathroom accessible only through my office so that no one else ever used it or even knew about it. The office was still not many steps from Paule's office, and it offered a pleasant setting for us to have a quiet tea and chat in my lounge area. This latter was only occasional because Paule spent very little time on campus after her classes and scheduled appointments.

THIS PICTURE WAS TAKEN MORE THAN THIRTY YEARS LATER, BUT THOUGH THE BOOKS AND FURNISHINGS ARE NOT THE SAME, THE CONFIGURATION HAS NOT CHANGED AND CLEARLY SHOWS THE UNIQUE "SUITE" I ENJOYED DURING MY LATER YEARS AT VCU.

OUR FRIENDSHIP

As I reflect for this memoir, I realize that ours was an unusual friendship—somewhat difficult to describe. It's not quite the friendship that Paule describes in "Reena," where the narrator tells us, "She [Reena] was... the lord and I the lackey" (*Reena and Other Stories* 73), for despite my almost worshipping of Paule, she was never one to lord it over anyone. Perhaps our friendship is best explained by comparison with Paule's friendship with Langston Hughes. Though Paule may never have realized this, I always viewed myself as the ardent fan in awe of her that she was to Hughes.

Paule opens TR with "Homage to Mr. Hughes," a recounting of her trip to Paris and varied other European sites with Langston Hughes, who had chosen the budding novelist to accompany him on a state-sponsored cultural tour of Europe in 1965. She often spoke movingly about that trip, as she did at the opening session of the remarkable 1992 "Afro Americans in Europe Conference" in Paris. That 1965 European tour with Hughes, especially the first part in Paris, was clearly the most memorable trip of all of her many, **many** travels—and her devotion to Hughes is one of her most adoring relationships. She delighted in his introducing her to his favorite haunts in Paris, his attentive guardianship during the trip, and his encouragement of her career. She clearly treasured the handwritten cards he sent her. She recalls his appearance at her first book signing: she was awed that the "great" man, the "handsome" man, the "poet-laureate of black America," "the literary icon" had "come to beam at me." (TR 3-4) She reproduces in TR the note he sent her in 1961 upon her publication of *Soul Clap Hands and Sing*, writing:

> A postcard arrived from Mr. Hughes, written in his distinctive green ink. "'Clap Hands' is about the prettiest looking book I ever saw," the card read. "It just now came. I look forward to reading it." His large boyish flourish of a signature at the bottom. (4)

Clearly, Hughes was to her what she was to me—a lionized, bigger-than-life celebrity writer whose friendship delighted and awed her. Though she always made a point of making sure that people pronounced her name properly, she would never correct **his** mispronunciation, even **liking** his insistence on pronouncing it "Paul-**ee**." And she,... she always reverentially referred to him as "**Mr.** Hughes" (emphasis mine). She even gladly accepted third-class accommodations in The California Hotel because it was where **Mr.** Hughes always stayed when in Paris.

Paule was a very private and reserved individual, and I was always careful not to in any way take advantage of our friendship to impose on her writing, her privacy, her celebrity, her renown, her reserve, her graciousness. I never even asked her to autograph any of her books—and I have **all** of her books. She did give me an **autographed** copy of the 1988 edition of *Soul Clap Hands and Sing* as a New Year's gift in 1989.

A note accompanying the book thanked me for an Olive Senior collection I had recently given her, and, referring to her

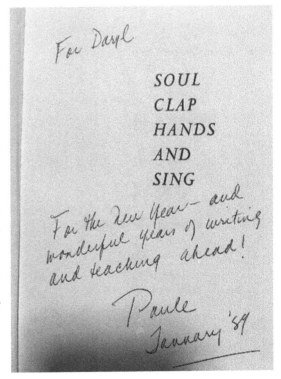

For Daryl

SOUL
CLAP
HANDS
AND
SING

For the New Year—and wonderful years of writing and teaching ahead!

Paule
January '89

book to me, Paule wrote: "Here's a little something for you—old, old wine in a new bottle—finally out from Howard Univ. Press. I never thought it would make it."

I treasure that autographed book!

I never even considered asking Paule to review a manuscript for me. Even though I finished the first drafts of my novels *Till Death Us Did Part* and *Land of the Free... Negroes* by 2008, I don't believe I even told Paule that I was trying my hand at fiction. In fact, one of the short stories in my collection, *Here Am I*, was inspired by a nightmare I had, in which I dreamed I heard on the tv that Paule had died. This was long before she had any ailments that I knew about. I never said a word about either the dream or the story to Paule. I am sure that had she known that I was trying my hand at fiction, she would have encouraged me and perhaps even expressed some interest in seeing my work. I am sure she would have given me some valuable hints to improve the novels. But I considered it an imposition to—in any way—take her away from **her** work.

Would I take Beethoven away from composing a masterpiece to listen to a little ditty I was composing!

Paule and I were friends. We were close friends. We were congenial friends. But we were not chums, we were not soul sisters, we were not confidants, we were not intimates. I am sure that during those years after she arrived in Richmond, we spent more time together than I spent with any other of my close, famous writer-friends, such as Nikki Giovanni, Erna Brodber, and Velma Pollard. In fact, I probably spent more time with Paule than with any of my other professional colleagues or other friends of any ilk: board, church, neighborhood, college, civic, club, sorority or bridge friends. We shared countless pleasant conversations, travels, meals, walks, friends, stories, and laughs. Indeed, Paule became a part of my family, sharing in most of our events from 1984 until my husband Warren's illness, beginning in 2009. Paule never just dropped by our house, but if she was not traveling, she always joined us whenever I invited her. Though I went to pick her up at her condo countless times, I could count on one hand the number of times I went in. I never ate a meal that Paule cooked. In fact, I don't even know if she liked to cook. That is not something I ever remember coming up in our discussions.[3] Notwithstanding, it is important to note that Paule entertained me a great deal; she loved planning events she knew I would enjoy, often capping them with a meal at one of her favorite or newly discovered restaurants.

Colleagues in the field, publishing companies, journal editors, students, and miscellaneous fans of Paule from all over the world certainly regarded me as her close friend, indeed as the authority on Paule, and as a possible entrée to Paule. From the time she came to Richmond, they overwhelmed me with requests to contact her, to have her speak, to interview her, to honor her, to review works related to her, to provide blurbs to works treating her, to get information about her, to seek details and explanations about her writing, to meet her. Typical was this inquiry, which began:

[I am] _____ from India. I am an Assistant professor of English in south India. I am very much interested in African American Literature especially Women's Writing. I would like to do my Ph.D. research work in Paule Marshall's novels. I tried to locate her contact address but couldn't locate her. (Email 10/13/2015)

I never gave personal information or contact details, always simply suggesting that inquirers write to Paule in the English Department at VCU (1984-94) and, later, to the English Department at New York University (hereafter, NYU) (1994-2018). Some people simply asked me to allow them to address something to Paule

---

[3] As I have been reflecting on our friendship during the development of this memoir, even I am amazed at the many ordinary things I never knew about Paule, especially given the time we spent together.

and send it to me to be passed on, a request I usually discouraged, though I did reluctantly (but hopefully) forward a letter from one impressive Emory scholar who was writing a promising book to Paule's home address in New York on August 26, 2007.

On rare occasions, I would cautiously directly pass on a request that I assumed Paule might not mind hearing about. On April 25, 2012, I passed on requests from a producer who wanted to option some of her work and from someone else who wanted to give her an award. I don't believe Paule responded to me about either of those messages, and I don't know if she got in touch with those people. If I passed on something to her once, I certainly wasn't going to follow up on it. In another instance, I mentioned a request that I felt certain she would respond to from one of our former VCU students who was working on a project. But I had no luck. I wrote back to our former student: "I'm sorry to say that Paule Marshall will not allow me to give out the contact information. I tried to make her remember you, but though the name sounded familiar, she did

HERE, PAULE AND I ARE PICTURED AT THE EVENT WITH CHARLES H. ROWELL AND JOSEPH SKERRETT

not. I explained that [a major journal] had asked you to interview her, but she said she simply wasn't up to that—not even to chat about the possibility" (April 16, 2013).

Some people probably gave me more credit than I deserved for helping them contact Paule, as in the following communication from Charles H. Rowell, the founder, and editor of *Callaloo*, the premier journal of literature, art, and culture of the African Diaspora. On August 29, 2007, he wrote to thank me for participating in the *Callaloo* 30th Anniversary Celebration:

Thank you very much for helping to get Paule Marshall to read; I know you were carefully working in the background, encouraging her to say "yes." Why? Because you always did (and do now) believe in CALLALOO. Thank you. Thank you.

I was certainly always a fan of *Callaloo* and its founder. And, as I note elsewhere, Paule and I had a great time at the *Callaloo* event.

And Martha E. Cook wrote to me on June 29, 1990: "So—could I impose on you and ask you to speak informally with Ms. Marshall and find out if she will agree to come to Longwood to receive the [Dos Passos] Prize?" I cautiously raised the subject with Paule, and she agreed to Martha's request. After continuing to consult with me while making all the plans for the Dos Passos award, Martha E. Cook wrote, "Once more, thanks for everything. You are certainly making my job easier" (9/21/1990).

Then there were the friends who simply mentioned Paule in passing to me, the way someone might say, "I saw your sister at the Spoonbread Restaurant[4] last night." Val Gray Ward, for example, wrote to thank me for a piece of my mother's usher uniform to include in her already-legendary quilt[5] and wrote at the top where she could find some space, "Oh, Yeah, Paule called" (undated note between 1990 and 2000). One student

---

4 A popular Richmond restaurant.
5 A student in Nikki Giovanni's class wrote after seeing the quilt, "Today I met Val Gray Ward. I asked her if she was an angel. She made us a quilt. She made the ancestors a quilt."

wrote just to tell me that she saw Paule at a restaurant and wanted to speak to her but was reluctant to interrupt her meal.

There were requests regarding Paule that did not require any intrusion upon the author, and I did respond to several. I provided cover blurbs for at least three books that focused on Paule: Dorothy Hamer Denniston, *The Fiction of Paule Marshall*. Knoxville: The University of Tennessee Press, 1995; Joyce Pettis, *Toward Wholeness in Paule Marshall's Fiction*. Charlottesville, The University Press of Virginia, 1995; and Elizabeth Brown-Guillory. *Middle Passages and the Healing Place of History*. Columbus: The Ohio State University Press, 2006 (this latter book includes essays on Morrison, Marshall, Aidoo, and Kincaid). Over the years, I reviewed a number of manuscripts of dissertations, essays, and books on or including Paule for individuals, publishing companies, and journals.

I also received several invitations to write an article on Paule, to agree to an interview focusing on her, and to appear on panels focusing on her and her work.

I agreed to only a very few of these requests over the years.

LEARNING ABOUT PAULE'S FAMILY / HER WRITING ABOUT THEM

Though Paule never shared any previously unrevealed family secrets during our talks, she often recounted a few familiar anecdotes about her parents, grandmother, and son. Many of those accounts are those that appear frequently in her books, speeches, and interviews. While she often denied that her work was autobiographical, she also admitted that aspects of her characters were influenced by herself and her family members.

Paule was born in Brooklyn, New York, on April 9, 1929, to Barbadian emigrants Ada and Samuel Burke. They named her Valenza Pauline.

She obviously adored Samuel Burke and grieved throughout her life what she viewed as her abandonment by her handsome father, something of a lady's man, who was forever hopelessly pursuing dreams that did not materialize, jumping from one disappointing job to another and then yet another, and vainly seeking a home. He had been born in Barbados, though Paule never learned just where in Barbados he was born nor the names of his parents; he spent some time in Cuba before becoming an illegal alien in the US; he continually dreamed of returning home to Barbados, but he never did. Finally, he deserted his family to join the Kingdom of Father Divine, leaving his wife and children in severe financial and emotional straits. Paule told me in our interview, "The greatest grief of my childhood was that my father **deserted** us to become a member of Father Divine's quasi-religious cult." She talks about her father in almost all of her interviews. He clearly is central in the development of Deighton Boyce, the father in *Brown Girl*, and Jerome Johnson (Jay), Avey's husband in *Praisesong for the Widow*.

Paule was forever in awe of her hard-working, determined, proud, and outspoken mother (referring in TR to her "Xanthippe voice" [94]), whose efforts were focused on winning "respect" and achieving her dreams of owning a brownstone. Paule frequently attributes her development as a writer and the finding of her voice to "the poets in the kitchen," those Caribbean expatriates who gathered with her mother around the kitchen table to reminisce about home and complain about their jobs. Paule's accounts of those conversations in a number of fictional works and speeches are among some of the best of her remarkable reproductions of Caribbean folk speech. A similar mother-figure, Silla Boyce, is the focus of *Brown Girl*, an early work that most critics consider the most autobiographical of Paule's novels.[6]

Paule was mesmerized by her grandmother, "M' Da-duh," whom she met only once—on her first trip to Barbados when she was seven. Her grandmother had sold some of her land to pay for the family's passage from New York to Barbados. The moment the young Paule saw the "juggernaut figure" of her grandmother (TR 70), she was awestruck and remained so throughout her life. Indeed M' Da-duh is everywhere in one form or another, in everything she has written, in every interview she has given, and in general conversations. Da-duh is **the** central figure in "one of her most beautiful stories, "To Da-duh, in Memoriam," which Paule declares "the most autobiographical of the stories [in "*Reena*" and Other Stories]" ("*Reena*" and Other Stories 95). She is undoubtedly the source of Mrs. Thompson in *Brown Girl*; Lessy Walker in *The Chosen Place*; Aunt

---

[6] Her early story, "Reena," is perhaps more autobiographical, with its narrator being a writer named Paulie. However, the story is more about the character Reena than the narrator Paulie. Commissioned by *Harper's Magazine*, it appeared in their special supplement on "The American Female" in October 1962. As noted elsewhere, Paule at one time told me that *Daughters* was perhaps her most "personal" novel. It is worth noting that Paule has suggested that her very first story, "The Valley Between," is autobiographical in its treatment of a young woman whose husband wants her to stay home and take care of the child. She indicates that she used white characters in that story "to camouflage my own predicament." ("*Reena*" and Other Stories" 15)

Cuney in *Praisesong for the Widow*; and Celestine and Congo Jane in *Daughters*. Of Da-duh, Paule told me during our interview,[7] "I have the feeling I was perhaps put here on this earth to preserve or continue her essence." In addition to those characters Paule mentioned above, other memorable portraits of elderly/ancestral figures include Florence Varina McCullum-Jones and Ulene Payne in *The Fisher King*. Some note might also be given to a significant male ancestral figure such as Lebert Joseph in *Praisesong for the Widow*.

Paule only rarely mentioned to me her sister, Anita Burke Wharton, who was four years older than she, but it was clear from occasional conversations that the sister was an important part of her life. There had been times that the sister kept her son for her, sometimes when Paule was away on extended trips. The sister occasionally visited her in Richmond, with Paule suggesting in TR that the sister, a heavy smoker, came to get cigarettes that were so much cheaper here that people smuggled contraband cigarettes from Virginia to New York. Paule painfully watched as heavy smoking led to her sister's breathing becoming more and more labored until, finally, she was no longer able to travel. Paule then supervised her care in New York, traveling frequently to oversee her maintenance and manage her business. Paule occasionally briefly mentioned her sister's problems to me. She noted on several occasions that she was going to New York to check on her or that she had just come back from visiting with her ailing sister.

. . . .

Then, she informed me of her death. Her sister died of pulmonary hypertension at 3:16 a.m. on October 6, 1995. Like many who have witnessed the painful suffering of the dying, Paule seemed during our conversation more relieved than distraught, and her reserved composure prevented me from offering the hug normally accorded a dear friend on such a sad occasion. I never knew enough about the sister to determine if any of Paule's characters seemed influenced by her, though the older sister, Ina Boyce, in *Brown Girl*, coincides with the age and position of Anita Burke Wharton in Paule's family. The relationship of the sisters is rarely a focus in *Brown Girl*, with Ina being the gentle and submissive minor character, one who might have in real life adjusted more easily to the early marriages that the sisters were encouraged to enter.

I don't ever recall that Paule shared any recollections of her brother with me, though she has often made it clear to me—and in several sources—that her parents were disappointed that Paule was a girl and later were elated at the appearance of a boy. Beyond that, Paule never, in my presence or in interviews that I can recall, spoke of her brother until she relates his birth nine years after her birth and his name, Franklin Edsel, in TR. Like her father, who "refused to ever speak of father, mother, sister or brother" (TR 109), Paule tells us nothing further about the brother—nothing more of him, even there. His only "appearance" in her fiction is in *Brown Girl*, where Selina (usually viewed as the fictional Paule) knows him only as her **deceased** brother, who died before she was born. Her only awareness of him is through a family picture of her mother, father, sister, and brother. Oddly enough, Selina's disdain for the brother stems from that picture, which is all that she knows about him:

"He's like a girl with all that hair," she muttered contemptuously. He had been frail and dying with a bad heart while she had been stirring into life. She had lain curled in the mother's stomach, waiting for his dying to be complete, she knew, peering through the pores as the box containing his body was lowered

---

[7] See "An Interview with Paule Marshall," *Southern Review* 28:1 (1992): 1-20; reprinted in James C. Hall and Heather Hathaway, *Conversations with Paule Marshall*. Jackson: UP of Mississippi, 2010. 96-115. I have used my copy of that interview for quotations here, so no page numbers appear in citations from that interview.

into the ground. Then she had come, strong and well-made, to take his place. But they had taken no photographs. (8)

Paule's abrupt dispatch of this despised brother in *Brown Girl* reminds us of Jamaica Kincaid's complete omission of her three brothers in her Bildungsroman *Annie John,* her jealousy of the favoritism accorded them, and her frequent uncharitable treatment of them in other works. Clearly, Marshall's and Kincaid's Caribbean culture, with its privileging of male children, made such jealousies inevitable.

Paule said little about her husbands during our chats, occasionally noting the political ambitions of one and the accidental death of the other but rarely naming them. She and her sister were pushed into early marriages, and it is clear that her writing was her major focus during what she described as "an early, unwise first marriage" (*"Reena" and Other Stories* 15) to a fellow New Yorker of Barbadian heritage, Kenneth Marshall, in 1950. He was a psychologist. Seven years after their divorce in 1963, she married Haitian businessman Nourry Ménard. I expect that the husband in *Daughters* is modeled in some ways after the Haitian husband. Clearly, a few anecdotes there seem based on him and his family.

She has indicated that both marriages were "open" (TR 98-99; Denniston 127).

Clearly, the joy of Paule's life was her brilliant, successful, and handsome son, Evan. Whenever there was some brief mention of him during our conversations, her eyes brightened up, and her smile broadened. Paule was eight months pregnant with Evan at the previously-mentioned book party launching her first book when Langston Hughes appeared to celebrate her achievement. The publication of *Brown Girl*, the birth of Evan, and the relationship with her literary idol are all frequently intertwined elements of the highlights of her life. When *Brown Girl* was accepted by Random House, her editor gave her an advance, specifically to "take this swollen, overwritten baby tome of yours and to extricate from it the slender, impressive first novel that's buried there" (TR 96). Paule would, through the years, refer to Evan as "the book party baby." One wonders if Viney's charming son Robeson in *Daughters* is influenced by Evan; if so, it is interesting that he is conceived by artificial insemination. I found him such an interesting and promising figure that I asked Paule during an interview if she might write about him in a later novel. She responded, "It's uncanny that you should ask that because, in the novel that's slow-ly-y beginning to take shape in my head now, there's a little boy who will figure as a central character"—thus giving me my first preview of *The Fisher King*, which came out in 2000. I expect there might be something of Evan in Sonny Payne, the charming international grandson of two feuding families, who is a central figure in *The Fisher King*.

Perhaps even more of a delight in Paule's life was the appearance of two grandchildren, Nina Prudence, and James Julius, truly a blessing to someone who never dreamed that her handsome bachelor son would ever give her grands. I remember when Paule announced the first grand to me. My always-composed friend was positively giddy as she pulled out a picture to show me. With the arrival of the second, she again pulled out a picture. (I don't remember Paule ever pulling out **any** other picture to show me!) They were late arrivals in her life, and the doting grandmother could not see enough of them, though it appeared that visits with her European grands were limited by distance, by her advancing age, and by other issues.

It was clear from early on that, like Zora Neale Hurston, Paule was a dedicated writer married to her craft, one for whom love was a pleasant aside but never paramount. Paule occasionally enjoyed male companionship and, even as a septuagenarian, liked having a proper male escort for certain events. But Paule relied on Paule. The personality traits that her mother saw in her were

"*Hard-ears!*"

"*Willful*!"

"Own Ways!" (TR 83-84)

Paule persisted, always in her "Own Ways!" Though her first husband[8] was pleased that she was a writer, she told Alexis DeVeaux that he objected to her spending time away to work on *Soul Clap Hands and Sing*, but she continued, "I went ahead and did it. There were, he sensed it, I knew it, my need and determination to be my own woman. To do my own thing."[9] I believe that from the moment her first novel was accepted by a major publisher, with an advance, and then won her a Guggenheim Award—through to a string of other awards, culminating in the MacArthur—Paule was fully committed to her work and confident of her place in American / African Diasporic / Caribbean / World literature.

PAULE, 1987

Always she remained, as she described herself to me in our interview:

Essentially I am someone who has always lived on the periphery wherever I am. I'm basically a loner, with a very limited social life, by choice; someone whose day is pretty much given over to the work.

Though Paule was an eloquent conversationalist, she often describes herself as silent and frequently makes a contrast between her silent women characters and those women characters who talk a great deal, even sometimes too much, wishing that she might have more of the personalities of the latter. When I asked her about the silence of some of the women in *Daughters* and their lack of communication with each other, she replied:

What you see as silence, or the refusal or inability of the key women in *Daughters* to express themselves verbally, is a technique I deliberately chose to employ. First of all, I felt that it was in keeping with the characters, their personalities. It also provided me with a chance to deal with the silence that so often characterized my own relationships. I used to find it exceedingly difficult to express what I truly felt with my partners. Perhaps the silence in *Daughters* comes out of that in part. I'm not sure. On the other hand, Merle in *Chosen Place*,[10] who talked nonstop [laughter], and Silla Boyce, the mother in *Brown Girl*, who loved to boast that she had no cover for her mouth and proved it on every page of the novel, [laughter][11] were idealized images for me, the kind of outspoken, assertive women I would've loved to have been. Also, the talk was in keeping with the kind of personalities I created for them. Avey Johnson in *Praisesong* and Ursa and Estelle in *Daughters* are perhaps closer to me in what you view as their silence. And I know it's a kind of outmoded response these days. People are not only supposed to talk endlessly but to divulge their most intimate feelings. I suspect, though, that silence is still true for a lot of women.

Some years later, in 2000, Paule gave us another talkative woman, Ulene Payne, who is here talking to her nine-year-old great-grandson, whom she has just met for the first time:

The woman going on and on, her voice a hurricane-force wind battering her slight, bowed frame, her rage desecrating her palais royal room. "Bet you're thinking I don't like this great- grandma. She talks too much." (*The Fisher King* 39-40)

---

[8] Kenneth Marshall, whom she married in 1950, when she was twenty-one, and divorced in 1963.
[9] "Paule Marshall: In Celebration of Our Triumph." *Essence Magazine* 10:1, 1979. 123.
[10] Merle declared, "And if I was to ever stop talking that'd be the end of me." (*The Chosen Place, The Timeless People*, 96).
[11] Both of us were collapsing in laughter by this time; tears were running down my face.

Certainly, the author's own silence, which she told me often impacted her relationships with men, is reflected in Ursa's relationship with Lowell in *Daughters*. That couple's relationship is restricted by many things, but basically by the fact that they never truly and openly talked to each other. What a different story it might have been if Ursa had told Lowell she was pregnant with his child!

OUR SUPPORT OF EACH OTHER

From the time we met, Paule and I supported each other's work. I often received letters and calls from individuals indicating that Paule had highly recommended my work to them. Professor Lee Potter of Wake Forest wrote a letter from England on March 27, 1986, to ask for particulars about my publications on West Indian writers: "I feel sure from what Ms. Marshall said about your book that it will be greatly helpful to me [as I prepare the first course offered in Wake Forest on Commonwealth literature]... I also look forward to meeting you someday." Professor Atsuko Furomoto, Professor of Afro-American Literature, Kobe College, Japan, wrote to me on March 26, 1992, "Ms. Paule Marshall, whom I met in New York in 1988 and again in Richmond in 1990, kindly advised me to ask you if I have questions concerning this field."

I eagerly took advantage of opportunities to initiate and support honors for her work.

As previously noted, on June 29, 1990, Professor Martha Cook wrote to formally inform me that Paule had been selected to receive the 1990 John Dos Passos Prize for Literature and to request that I informally find out if she would come to Longwood College in Farmville, VA, to receive the prize. If Paule answered in the affirmative, a formal letter would be sent to her. She went on to ask me to come and introduce Ms. Marshall. She closed with a request for Ms. Marshall's address. I sent her Paule's VCU address.

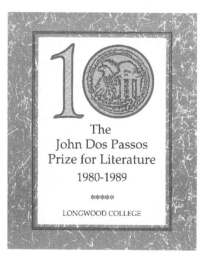

On the big day of the award (October 9, 1990), I picked Paule up, and we drove to Longwood. Because of my role (I had nominated her and was scheduled to introduce her), I received the same first-class treatment that was accorded Paule Marshall at the Award Ceremonies—a letter from the College President, Bill Dorrill, welcoming me to the event and to dinner with him beforehand and offering me the opportunity to decide if I wanted to stay for coffee and chats with the guests or go for a rest before the event. It was a big evening for Paule, who had joined a long list of distinguished recipients of the Dos Passos Award. It was a big evening for me: I was a part of all events, I introduced Paule, and my comments about Paule appeared in the program. Indeed, Martha requested a copy of my introduction "for the record, and perhaps a quote next year" (letter, Feb. 8, 1991).

On August 28, 1991, I received a letter from Mary Ann Worklan: "Paule Marshall has been nominated for a MacArthur Fellowships. On behalf of our Selection Committee, I am writing to ask you for your confidential evaluation of the nominee's qualifications."

Ms. Worklan provided the nomination, a beautifully prepared nomination by another ardent Marshall aficionado. I could not help but note that he had made one claim that was debatable: "She has never had both freedom from financial worry and the time in which to write." Paule actually received an advance on her first novel that allowed her to spend almost a year in Barbados revising it. Then in 1962, she received a Guggenheim, which she described as "the most generous and prestigious literary prize after the famous Pulitzer" (TR 120), one that allowed her to rent a house in Grenada, hire a nanny for her son, a housekeeper, a cook, and a handyman; and settle down to write for almost a year, during which she spent most of the day writing while reserving evenings on the beach with her son.[12]

Nonetheless, I was one of those fans who believe that an artist like Paule can never have enough time and enough wherewithal to commit herself to her craft without **any** worry about money or child, or time. Never did I work so hard with so much enthusiasm to make the case that no one more than Paule deserved (in the words of the MacArthur Fellows Program) "[financial support] for five years" to provide the recipients "a release from constraints... and enable them to do original work of any kind and of their own choosing" (letter from The John and Catherine MacArthur Foundation, August 28, 1991).

I also suggested, as requested, another possible reviewer to them.

I never mentioned any of my communications with the MacArthur Foundation to Paule.

Paule received the MacArthur Fellowship in the summer of 1992 to local, national, and international acclaim. It was the top front-page event in *The Richmond Times Dispatch*...

VCU PROFESSOR WINS $369,000 AWARD

where she was reported to have declared to the reporter, "Oh, what a glorious day this has been.... I am soaring." The University was ecstatic, even President Eugene P. Trani, who had told me in no uncertain terms several years prior that there "will never be an African American Studies [major] while I am President." He proclaimed to the reporter that Paule was "a treasure for us here at VCU" (*Times Dispatch* article by Gary Robertson). Paule received an award of $369,000 plus health insurance.

Several of our friends, including noted writers, wrote to me to express their delight that Paule had won the MacArthur.

Despite my reluctance to personally request any favors from Paule, I enjoyed a number of benefits resulting from our relationship. I allowed my publishers to make some requests on my behalf. I remain grateful that among other favors, in 1998, she allowed the reproduction of a scene from *Brown Girl, Brownstones* ("Talk Yuh Talk") in my *Honey, Hush!* (154-55) and she graciously provided the following blurb for *Honey, Hush!*

---

[12] Paule's determination to allow a special time for her son each day and her recognition that "It has not been easy for my son, being the child of a mother who writes" (interview with Alexis DeVeaux, 45) is reproduced in Hattie in *The Fisher King*, who determined to take time out of her busy day to take her young charge Sonny out for a walk: "The daily stroll took place even in the rain." Their daily ritual ended with the purchase of a baguette that they started eating as they returned home and she left for her evening job (59-63). Hattie is an important figure to me as I am remembering Paule, for *The Fisher King* is built around Hattie remembering her musical idol, Sonny-Rett Payne.

In an extraordinary display of literary research, Daryl Dance has assembled a treasure trove of black womanist humor that attests to our transcendent power to overcome and to survive.

In 2002, she allowed the reproduction of a passage from *Praisesong for the Widow* in my *From My People: 400 Years of African American Folklore* (597).

Clearly, being Paule's friend provided me a special entrée into any number of exclusive groups, events, and places.

PAULE AND ME

During our trip to Howard University (March 3-5, 1995) for the establishment of The Sterling A. Brown Chair, my longtime friend Barbara Glenn and I were invited along with Paule to the private events following the grand program, beginning with Eleanor Traylor's reception at her house for Toni Morrison, Toni Cade Bambara, and Paule Marshall. What a delightful evening! What memorable stories! Morrison was front and center, bringing us to tears and laughter as she recounted the fire at her home and as she told about deciding on her outfit and her hair style for the Nobel Laureate presentation. The next morning, we all went to James Baldwin's mother's home in D.C. for brunch. How honored I was not only to meet Baldwin's mother and sister but to enjoy their delicious cooking and hear them share stories of their famous son/brother, who was a friend of Toni, Toni, and Paule![13] (James Baldwin was also an acquaintance of mine, whom I had invited and whom I had introduced at readings at VCU and the University of California at Santa Barbara.) I had had opportunities on individual occasions to wine and dine, laugh and joke, and listen to reflections on literature from Morrison, Bambara, and Marshall, but never was there such a glorious opportunity to be practically a part of the Triumvirate of celebrated African American novelists letting their hair down and celebrating each other and other literary greats.

---

[13] So many of us around during the African American Writers Renaissance had "male" names. The Tonies and Paule had modified their given names, but mine appears on my birth certificate.

PAULE IS WITH WINTERGREEN SISTERS OPAL MOORE AND
JOANNE GABBIN

I would later, in 2012, have the honor of being the first professor appointed to the Sterling A. Brown Chair.

As much as Paule and I traveled together, we each always had our private rooms in the hotels in which we stayed. I don't think either of us would have considered having a roommate. In most instances, of course, Paule, as the distinguished guest, was given fine accommodations by her host. From my upbringing as an only child, I was never accustomed to sharing a room. Indeed, several of my professional and bridge friends joke about the fact that I refuse to share rooms when we travel.

When Paule learned that I was going to Barbados in 1995 to serve as an external reviewer of the English Department at the University of the West Indies (hereafter UWI), Cave Hill, she immediately sent off a letter of introduction to her friend, Carolyn Marie Plaskett Barrow. Mrs. Barrow, the widow of the first and fourth Prime Minister of Barbados,[14] was a fascinating personage in her own right. A native of New Jersey, she was educated at Oberlin and went on to study fine arts in New York, Paris, and Denmark. At Paule's behest, she welcomed and entertained me in Barbados. Not only did she host me at dinner and show me around Barbados, but my prestige among my UWI associates was greatly enhanced by simply mentioning in passing that I had, just yesterday, enjoyed dinner with Mrs. Barrow and that Paule Marshall was my colleague at VCU.

Though it is difficult to be a scholar of twentieth-century African American literature without treating Paule, I was reluctant to focus on her works in my academic writing, and I circumspectly avoided requesting assistance from her in analyzing, critiquing, or writing about her work.[15] The one exception to my self-imposed constraint was spearheaded by Dave Smith, a colleague who had worked with us at VCU before moving on to serve as editor of the *Southern Review*. In 1991 Dave asked me to do an interview with Paule regarding her forthcoming novel, *Daughters*. I explained to him that I was reluctant to ask her for an interview, so he took care of securing her permission and arranging for the interview.

The interview was conducted in her condo on June 14, 1991. *Daughters* would appear in the Fall of 1991.

As always, I was cautious about posing any questions that might cross any boundaries and feared there might be some awkwardness in presuming to explore her motivations, methods, characterization, etc., with her. Surprise of surprises, the interview was like our regular, frequent conversations, with both of us soon unaware of the tape recorder and actually enjoying the exchange, so much so that before I knew it, Paule was mentioning a never-before-revealed rape. I had asked her about the abortion in *Daughters*, and she replied with this shocking addendum: "Writing about the abortion in the story was also personally therapeutic. Writing about it permitted me to deal for the first time with a similar trauma in my own life when I was a

14 Earl Barrow served from 1966-1976 and was reelected in 1986. He died in 1987.
15 However, I often jokingly said to her when I was having difficulty with contributors promptly submitting their essays for my *Fifty Caribbean Writers: A Bio-Bibliographical Critical Sourcebook*, that I might be forced to write an essay on her to reach the magic number (50!).

young woman. A date rape, an unwanted pregnancy, a back-alley abortion, which was the only kind available in my day." I was careful not to persist with further questions, but she was open and added a few details, seemingly relieved to finally mention this painful event. This interview was one of our most open and free discussions of private, intimate personal histories. I was careful to give her a copy of the transcribed interview for reviews and corrections to assure that she had an opportunity to delete some information after she had time to reflect on it. She made no changes.

Actually, on later reflections, considering all I know about Paule, I wouldn't be surprised if she had not indeed determined that our interview was the opportunity for her to mention that incident. She was not the kind of individual who let things slip out in the heat of the moment.

On further later reflections, I have also been surprised at the way I reacted to the revelation that my friend had been raped. Ordinarily, upon such a disclosure, I would immediately commiserate with a dear friend, offer some consolations, hug her or at least reach for her hand and squeeze it tight. But Paule's revelation was so clinical, so analytical, so impersonal that I simply sat there at the recorder, the calm, unflappable interviewer.

The interview was edited and submitted. When I received the information about the forthcoming interview in the Winter 1992 issue, the assistant editor, Donna Perreault, added a P.S.:

> Just a note from the Asst. Editor: I love the interview and tried to persuade Dave to keep in all the signs of friendship between you and Ms. Marshall. To no avail. He took the laughter out, but it remains a very strong interview and in fact is the lead-off piece of the issue!

Even with a few minor contributions to Marshall scholarship, such as that successful and often-cited interview, I do not consider myself a Marshall scholar. Indeed, I might more accurately be described as more or less a disciple, studying her, traveling with her, supporting her, teaching her work, and grooming and supporting other Marshall scholars. I taught her work every year that I taught AA lit or women writers at VCU and UR. I invited her on at least one occasion (Dec. 4, 1985) to visit one of my classes at VCU when we were discussing *Praisesong*. She also visited my class at UR in November or December 1992. Many of the students in my classes at VCU and UR went on to do research on Paule and to teach her works. On April 2, 2005, Melanie Clore wrote to me:

> I think of you often as I'm currently teaching an elective to my 11th and 12th graders built around *Annie John* and *Praisesong for the Widow*. My students hear about you all the time as I pass down the knowledge you taught me. It is really cool to be teaching Walcott, Marshall, and others in a school in NYC knowing that THEY are teaching or writing just a few blocks away.

From 1984 when Paule arrived in Richmond, until a few years before her death, she and I traveled together to professional events all over Richmond, Virginia, and beyond, some of them featuring either or both of us. We became so much a traveling duo that when one of us appeared at a local event, she was asked where the other was.[16] I became almost legendary as her introducer in Virginia circles and as a joint participant at her local presentations. There are clearly some events that I have forgotten, but the following are those noted in a letter, a program, a picture, a news account in my files, or my calendars (these latter impaired by the fact that I no longer have calendars before 1993).

On February 21, 1986, we read from our works at Richmond's Amber Gallery, 17 West Main Street.[17]

Marshall, Dance readings feature latest fiction

Authors Paule Marshall and Daryl C. Dance read from their work at Richmond's Amber Gallery, Feb. 21. Marshall, a VCU professor of English from 1984 to 1985, is taking this year off to work on a novel. Dance is currently an associate professor of English at the univeristy.

Marshall read from *Praise Song for the Widow*, her latest novel which describes the homecoming of a black woman and her heritage.

Dance described her work as the result of a group talent "from Jamaica, the U.S. and Africa." Her readings included a story about a slave named John who beat a drum to the tune of "do good." John's owner tries to poison the slave with con-taminated cake and water. Unknowingly, John gives the poisoned gift to his owner's two sons, who die as a result. The owner, his wife and maid all die of grief. The moral, according to tradition, is "if you dig a hole for a man, dig one for you and one for him."

Dance is author of *Folklore from Contemporary Jamaicans* and *Shuckin' and Jivin': Folklore from Contemporary Black Americans*.

Marshall is best known for *Brown Girl, Brownstones* and *Praisesong for the Widow*. The writer will return to teach fiction at VCU in 1987.

—*Brian Quess*

Commonwealth Times
March 4-24, 1986

Paule read from *Praisesong*; I read from *Folklore from Contemporary Jamaicans*. The program, sponsored by The Media Society, was followed by a reception for Paule and me.

---

[16] Of course, throughout Paule's Richmond years (1984-2019), the thirty-five years that she maintained a home in Richmond, each of us also separately promoted our books, lectured, and participated in conferences throughout the US, and in the Caribbean, Canada, Europe, Africa, Russia, and Japan. During the Richmond Years, Paule published *Merle: A Novella and Other Stories, Daughters, The Fisher King, Triangular Road*, and a new edition of *Soul Clap Hands and Sing*. During that time I published twelve books.

[17] Paule was on leave at the time.

THE MEDIA SOCIETY

Cordially Invites You To A

Reception Honoring

PAULE MARSHALL
Author of *Brown Girl , Brownstones*, et. al.

and

DR. DARYL DANCE
Author of *Folklore from Contemporary Jamaicans*, et. al.

Friday, February 21, 1986

THE AMBER GALLERY

17 West Main Street
Richmond, Virginia

6:30 PM – 8:30 PM
(7:15 PM – Selected Readings by Authors)

R.S.V.P. (regrets only): Lynn Rivers, (w) 780-1701, (h) 732-1788

On October 2, 1987, I drove her and colleague Opal Moore to Wintergreen for the first gathering of what would later be coined "The Wintergreen Collective." JMU Professor Joanne Gabbin had invited Virginia Fowler, Carmen Gillespie, Sandra Govan, Mary Harper, Trudier Harris, Paule Marshall, Opal Moore, Catherine Rogers, and me to The Wintergreen Resort in the Blue Ridge Mountains of Virginia to welcome Nikki Giovanni to Virginia.

What a memorable assembly of students, writers, and literary scholars! What a rejuvenating gathering of Black women from varied universities, grateful for the opportunity to meet, greet, share readings and projects, exchange experiences, and just plain enjoy each other's company!

JMU student Catherine Rogers, Paule Marshall, Nikki Giovanni, Daryl Dance, Joanne Gabbin, and Opal Moore

One of the early memorable events of the retreat was our rushing to see Nikki arriving in her new "candy-apple-red, five-speed Toyota MR2" (Nikki's description in *Shaping Memories* [6]). We enjoyed our first Wintergreen Reading. "The Reading," during which the writers shared and critiqued works in progress, remained the highlight of all of our future meetings. A few of us enjoyed a dip in the pool. Several gathered around a bid whist table to cheer on a heated match between Nikki and Ginney vs. Sandy and me. (Occasionally, Opal or Joanne also partnered with either Sandy or me at later whist matches.) At one point during our first Wintergreen retreat, we all dashed to the patio sliding glass doors to glimpse a new visitor—a large brown bear! A highlight of each day from this first meeting onward was gathering around our communal table to enjoy great meals and inspiring conversation. Individual writers were interviewed during both days of the first retreat by Rogers and Gillespie, the two JMU students. During breaks, there was recorded music; and occasionally, led by Joanne, we burst into song. And, oh, what exchanges of stories and tales of our experiences, our families, our universities, our classes, our battles! And then there were the daily walks, challenged by the snow on our second day. Here, Paule was at the forefront of the challenging mountain treks at Wintergreen. Joanne recalled in an email to the Wintergreen Sisters on August 2019, announcing Paule's demise:

> [T]he image that is indelible in my memory is Paule's stride in her brown velvet athletic suit as she beats us all to the Summit at the Wintergreen Resort on a cool autumn morning in September 1987.[18] Even though many of us had longer legs and more athletic bodies, we were no match for the agility and stamina of this petite woman who relished nature and exuded good health. . . . I will always remember our first gathering at Wintergreen and Paule's warmth and regal bearing.

---

[18] It was actually October.

Some of the brave walkers were almost blown away by that record blizzard of October 3, 1987. Nonetheless, we set out to enjoy dinner at a restaurant that night. It was a delightful meal, but blinded by fog, we feared we would never find our way back to our house. Indeed, Nikki and Ginney did not manage to get back until the next day.

There is no way anyone could ever anticipate the friendships, the legends, and yes, perhaps, the occasional inevitable lies that had their birth on this dramatic weekend. Looking back, it is hard to believe so many events were crammed into a weekend, and yet we all, on Sunday, October 4, left relaxed and rested.

As we cleared our rooms and packed our cars to say goodbye, we were already planning our next get-together. This was an experience that needed to be repeated—with additional writer friends. Over the years, scores of other writers have shared in the Wintergreen experience, including, one year or another, Mari Evans, Toi Derricotte, Pinkie Gordon Lane, Nikky Finney, Gloria Naylor, Val Gray Ward, Lucinda Roy, Karla Holloway, Eugenia Collier, Sonica Sanchez, Ethel Morgan Smith, Maryemma Graham, Hermine Pinson-- and the list goes on and on. Most of the first attendees remained regulars, and a few of us brought along family and friends on at least one occasion. Nikki's mother and sister attended one year, and my college classmate, Elaine Crocker, attended another year. When one of our retreats conflicted with my daughter Daryl Lynn's birthday, Joanne and I decided to bring our daughters, both of whom have regularly come back. Despite their advancing age, Daryl Lynn and Nayo are still labeled "The Wintergreen Daughters."

Though Paule did not attend any later meetings of The Wintergreen Collective, she did respond in 2009 to appeals from Joanne Gabbin and me to contribute to the Wintergreen collection, *Shaping Memories: Reflections of African American Women Writers*.

It is a sad coincidence that the first deaths among the original Wintergreen women were the oldest and the youngest of our first retreatants: Paule Marshall died on August 12, 2019, at the age of ninety, and Carmen Gillespie died on August 30, 2019, at the age of fifty-four.

Kindred Spirits

Wintergreen Writers Launch New Book

By Daryl Cumber Dance

First Wintergreen Retreat, October, 1987, pictured from left to right in the front row: Catherine Rodgers, James Madison University student; Daryl Cumber Dance and Opal Moore; back row from left to right: Paule Marshall, Nikki Giovanni, and Joanne Veal Gabbin.

In 1987, Joanne Veal Gabbin invited a group of ten writers, professors, and students to the Wintergreen Resort in the Blue Ridge Mountains of Virginia to welcome Nikki Giovanni, who had just joined the faculty at Virginia Polytechnic University in Blacksburg, Virginia. The weekend was so stimulating and inspirational that we decided to come together again the next year, and then the next, and the next, until now we have met for 22 consecutive years.

Though nearly every year there has been at least one new writer with us, there are core group members who have been to almost all of our meetings: Joanne Veal Gabbin, Sandra Y. Govan, Opal Moore, Trudier Harris, Daryl Cumber Dance, and Carmen R Gillespie. Gillespie, who attended our first meeting as a James Madison University student, literally grew up in Wintergreen; we have proudly watched her blossom as a prolific author, popular professor, and award-winning scholar.

Wintergreen daughters, Daryl Lynn Dance and Jessea Nayo Gabbin, have been with us since they were in high school. We are a body of kindred spirits who relish the opportunity to share our writing, our teaching, our projects, our events, our ideas with a group of active and talented writers who offer us guidance, understanding, new ideas, encouragement, and challenges. Numerous books, projects, and events that are now a part of America's literary history were conceived, planned, and/or refined around the dinner table at Wintergreen — or Williamsburg, or Barbados, or the Outer Banks of North Carolina, for we occasionally journey to other venues for our meeting.

This year, for example, from June 25-28, 2009, we met in Charlotte, North Carolina, in order to launch a book of personal essays focusing on the things that shaped us and our writing. Edited by Joanne Veal Gabbin, the book, *Shaping*

Wintergreen in Charlotte, June 28, 2009. Back row, l-r: Joanne Veal Gabbin, Daryl Cumber Dance, Virginia Fowler, Karla F.C. Holloway, and Joyce Pettis. Second row: Marilyn Sanders Mobley, Nikki Giovanni, Linda Williamson Nelson, and Sandra Govan. Front row, Val Gray Ward.

Memories: Reflections of African American Women Writers, is published by the University Press of Mississippi. Twelve of the Wintergreen women went to the University of North Carolina at Charlotte to read for the launching: Carmen R. Gillespie, Daryl Cumber Dance, Ethel Morgan Smith, Joyce Pettis, Mari Evans, Karla F.C. Holloway, Linda Williamson Nelson, Marilyn Sanders Mobley, Joanne Veal Gabbin, Opal Moore, Nikki Giovanni, and Sandra Y. Govan. The moving accounts of families and friends, loves and friendships, births and deaths, battles and victories, moved the audience from laughter to tears and from outrage to celebration.

The reception following the reading offered the Wintergreen writers the opportunity to interact with students, writers, professors, and readers from the Charlotte area and beyond, all of whom had interesting responses to our accounts as well as fascinating stories of their own. It was a memorable evening.

Other Wintergreen women who contributed to *Shaping Memories* are Paule Marshall, Kendra Hamilton, Elizabeth Brown-Guillory, Janus Adams, Camille Dungy, Maryemma Graham, Nikky Finney, Trudier Harris, Lovalerie King, Hermine Pinson, Eugenia Collier, Sonia Sanchez, and Toi Derricotte.

The Wintergreen in Charlotte gathering was full of interesting activities, beginning with Nikki Giovanni's reading from *Hip Hop Speaks to Children* on Thursday night and ending with an evening of good food, music, conversation, and review at Casa Govan, the home of our Charlotte one-woman host committee and planner.

Interspersed throughout were gatherings for informal discussions and heated debates, shopping trips, spa treatments, games, and tasty meals at our resort and other local restaurants. We bade each other a sad adieu on Sunday morning after a breakfast where we made plans for a couple of additional book readings during the school year and for our annual meeting in 2010. We are considering Virginia Beach or a return to Wintergreen, our original site which gave us our name.

We have often reflected upon the appropriateness of our name, which also calls to mind the flavoring, aromatic, and

healing qualities of the wintergreen plant. In her poem commemorating our tenth anniversary, "green in winter," Opal Moore celebrated our Wintergreen retreats as a ritual of healing and renewal:

Green in Winter

(Lines from poem used by permission of Opal Moore.)
They come,
The women wearing white
to gather on the mountain.

It is a summoning.
The women have prepared for this —
shed their hard shoes, rinsed their faces
and the soft folds
of winter feet in water chamomiled.
They eat mint leaves, and laughter,
make songs to welcome themselves back
from the wilderness and wars.

Here upon the mountain dreaming of ocean,
they are the joining,
they are the waking green
of winter.

For additional information on *Shaping Memories: Reflections of African American Women Writers* edited by Joanne Veal Gabbin, visit http://www.upress.state.ms.us/.

MY ABOUT TIME REVIEW OF SHAPING MEMORIES.

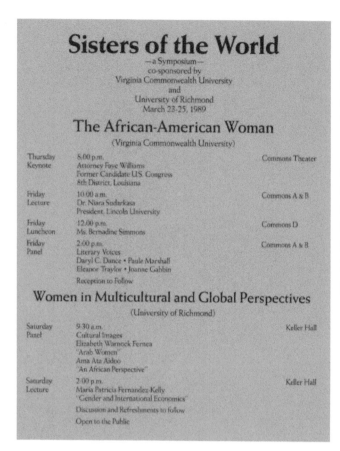

Sisters of the World
—a Symposium—
co-sponsored by
Virginia Commonwealth University
and
University of Richmond
March 23-25, 1989

The African-American Woman
(Virginia Commonwealth University)

Thursday Keynote	8:00 p.m. Attorney Faye Williams Former Candidate U.S. Congress 8th District, Louisiana	Commons Theater
Friday Lecture	10:00 a.m. Dr. Niara Sudarkasa President, Lincoln University	Commons A & B
Friday Luncheon	12:00 p.m. Ms. Bernadine Simmons	Commons D
Friday Panel	2:00 p.m. Literary Voices Daryl C. Dance • Paule Marshall Eleanor Traylor • Joanne Gabbin Reception to Follow	Commons A & B

Women in Multicultural and Global Perspectives
(University of Richmond)

Saturday Panel	9:30 a.m. Cultural Images Elizabeth Warnock Fernea "Arab Women" Ama Ata Aidoo "An African Perspective"	Keller Hall
Saturday Lecture	2:00 p.m. Maria Patricia Fernandez-Kelly "Gender and International Economics" Discussion and Refreshments to follow Open to the Public	Keller Hall

On March 24, 1989, Paule and I appeared on a panel along with Eleanor Traylor and Joanne Gabbin at Virginia Commonwealth University, part of a three-day symposium, "Sisters of the World," sponsored by VCU and UR.

On April 8, 1989, Paule and I appeared, along with African writers Ama Ata Aidoo and Es'kia Mphahlele, at the UR Symposium on "African and African Writers and Their Communities" in The Keller Hall Reception Room. Following the arrival of Mphahlele on April 7, Uliana G. Gabara, Head of International Studies at the University of Richmond, invited Paule, a few other participants, and me to have dinner with him.

**OFFICE OF INTERNATIONAL EDUCATION
UNIVERSITY OF RICHMOND
PRESENTS A SYMPOSIUM**

AFRICAN AND AFRICAN-AMERICAN WRITERS AND THEIR COMMUNITIES

SATURDAY, APRIL 8, 1989, KELLER HALL RECEPTION ROOM

PARTICIPANTS :

AMA ATA AIDOO, Ghanaian writer-in-residence, UR

DARYL DANCE, Specialist in African-American folklore and literature, VCU

PAULE MARSHALL, Novelist and short story writer, VCU

ES'KIA MPHAHLELE, South African writer, Fulbright scholar

MODERATOR: **LOUIS TREMAINE,** Specialist in African Literature, UR

Check-in: 9:30 AM, Coffee and doughnuts
Session I: 10:00 - 11:30 AM
Lunch: 11:45 - 1:00 PM (available for purchase at the Dining Hall)
Session II: 1:30 - 3:00 PM

**This event is free and open to the public
It is sponsored by a grant from the AT&T Foundation**

PLEASE POST

I was one of the speakers at Governor L. D. Wilder's "Virginia's African Trade Conference" in Williamsburg, Virginia, on November 19-20, 1990, an event planned by Esther Vassar, Paule's and my mutual friend and colleague. I drove down on the 19th; I believe, though I'm not certain, that Paule (who I know was invited) rode with me.

PAULE AND ESTHER AT EITHER WILDER'S AFRICAN TRADE CONFERENCE
OR HIS VCU EVENT WITH AFRICAN AMBASSADORS. PICTURE COMPLIMENTS OF ESTHER VASSAR.

On Sunday, December 2, 1990, Paule and I were Guest Lecturers at the closing reception of the VCU Black Caucus's Kwanzaa 90 at the Commons Theatre. The Moderator was Esther Vassar.

KWANZAA '90 PROGRAM OUTLINE

Theme: "NIA— Education Through Celebration"

Wednesday, November 28

Opening Ceremony/Reception	6:00 – 7:30 pm	Commons Theatre
Moderator/Presentor:	Rodney Pulliam	

Reception hosted by
Kappa Alpha Psi Fraternity, Eta Xi Chapter

Friday, November 30

Vendors	10:00 am – 4:00 pm	Commons Area
P.J. Gibson - Playwright	6:00 – 7:00 pm	Commons Room A

(Co-sponsored with VCU English Department)

Kwanzaa Dance	9 pm – 1 am	Cary Street Gym
	$ 1 African Dress	
	$ 2 VCU Students	
	$ 3 All Others (College ID)	

Saturday, December 1

Dr. Jawanza Kunjufu	10:30 am – Noon	
	1:00 – 2:30 pm	Business Building Aud.

"Raising the African American Consciousness
Through Culture"
"How to Raise the African American Boy to Manhood"

(Co-sponsored with the Office of Minority Student Affairs)

Saturday, December 1 Con't.

Unity Workshop	12:30 – 1:30 pm	Commons Room A
Moderator/Presentor:	Ishmail Conway, Assistant Director, Student Activities	
Vendors	1:00 – 7:00 pm	Commons Area
		Food, jewelry, clothing, books, etc.
Hair Designs	1:30 – 2:15 pm	Common Ground
		Featuring "BEAU"
		Carlton's Concepts/Hair Designs
Student Expression Variety Show	2:00 – 3:00 pm	Commons Theatre
		"Not a Competition"
Band Performance	3:00 – 6:00 pm	Park Place Lobby
		Itadi Bonney and First World

Sunday, December 2

Lecture and Closing Reception	2:00 – 5:30 pm	Commons Theatre

"The Readings and Reflections of Women of Words"

Moderator:	Esther Vassar
Guest Lecturers:	Paule Marshall
	Daryl Cumber Dance
Presentations:	Johari Players
	*EZIBU MUNTU African Dance Company

(Co-sponsor: Delta Sigma Theta Sorority, Eta Tau Chapter)

KWANZAA '90

Virginia Commonwealth University
Black Caucus

NOVEMBER 28 - DECEMBER 2

Theme: "NIA — Education
Through Celebration"

Program

RECOGNITION OF OUTSTANDING ACHIEVEMENT

Elske v.P. Smith, Dean
College of Humanities and Sciences

STUDENTS

DISTINGUISHED TEACHER AWARD
Walter R. Coppedge
Professor of English

DISTINGUISHED SCHOLARSHIP AWARD
Marcel Cornis-Pop
Associate Professor of English

LECTURE
"The Making of a Novel"
Paule Marshall
Professor of English

Introduction by Daryl C. Dance
Professor of English

OUTSTANDING ALUMNI AWARD
Jackson E. Jeffrey
B.S., Applied Science, 1954
Ph.D., Anatomy, 1964

On April 10, 1991, I introduced Paule, who was guest lecturer at the VCU College of Humanities and Sciences' Awards Ceremony; her topic was "The Making of a Novel."

On November 19, 1991, I introduced Paule when she read from *Daughters* at VCU. In that introduction, written as I was preparing to retire from VCU at the end of the school year, I suggested that my greatest legacy during my twenty years at VCU was making the call that led to bringing her to our university: "Yes, I **called**— I **dialed**—Paule Marshall. And that was a call that affected in no small way the history of this university and of American letters."

On Feb. 19, 1992, Paule and I were honored along with other colleagues at VCU's African American Alumni Council's Black History Month Reception Honoring VCU Faculty in Arts and Literature in the Anderson Gallery. The honorees are pictured here.

IN THE BACK ROW: CHRISTOPHER BROOKS, ALEXANDER BOSTIC, ROBERT "BOB" FOSTER, AND DONALD "DON" EARLEY; IN THE FRONT ROW: DARYL DANCE, REGENIA PERRY, LYDIA THOMPSON BOSTIC, MURRY DEPILLARS, SANDRA WILKINS; JANUS WATSON, AND PAULE MARSHALL.

On September 20, 1992, Paule and I were among numerous women honored at the Annual Women's Day of the Koinonia Independent Methodist Church. (I don't think either of us was able to attend.)

On October 13, 1992, I spoke at Virginia Tech. My subject was "'And What You Is?' Paule Marshall's Treatment of Children of Immigrants in *Brown Girl, Brownstones.*" Mrs. Julia Staples wrote me on Oct. 15, 1992: "I want to thank you for the splendid review of *Brown Girl, Brown Stones* you gave here on the 13th. It is by far the best review of any book I have heard in over 35 years." I also presented a version of that speech at a program sponsored by the Virginia State Library and The Virginia Foundation for the Humanities and Public Policy in Senate Room B, General Assembly Building in Richmond, VA, on October 22, 1992.

In 1992, Paule and I were invited by noted French scholar Michel Fabre to participate in the African Americans in Europe International Conference, Universite de Paris III: Sorbonne Nouvelle, Paris, France (held February 5-9), she to be the Keynoter at the opening session, and I to chair a session and serve as a respondent in a workshop. Paule opened the conference with recollections of her earlier US-Sponsored trip to Paris with Langston Hughes.

In her usual carefully organized manner, Paule determined that she and I should spend one afternoon of our Paris trip together, visiting the special haunts of Hughes and other Black American expatriates. We visited the bars and homes and hotels and general hangouts, I being, like the earlier Paule, the naïve American visitor, and Paule being my Langston Hughes, determined to help me understand and appreciate the Paris my tour guide adored. One highlight was enjoying a cocktail at Les Deux Magots. Paule, as always, ordered a kir. So enthused[19] was I to be at this iconic brasserie with Paule Marshall (and the spirits of so many others), I have no recollections of what I ordered. Here this little country girl from Charles City, VA, was seated at this legendary Café with **Ms**. Paule Marshall: the Café where Richard Wright and James Baldwin met and began their often-bitter quarrel about *Native Son*; the Café where Ernest Hemingway wrote *The Sun Also Rises*; the favorite stomping ground of Chester Himes and Langston Hughes, not to mention Jean-Paul Sartre, Pablo Picasso, and James Joyce. I, like Dante in Limbo, felt astounded to be admitted into such a select historical company.

JOANNE GABBIN, DARYL DANCE, PAULE MARSHALL, AND EVAN MARSHALL IN PARIS

On another day, following the dedication of a plaque at 14 rue Monsieur le Prince, an apartment that had long been the home of Richard Wright and his family, Paule, Joanne Gabbin, and I enjoyed lunch with Mrs. Richard Wright, her daughter, and grandson, and several other notables attending the conference, such as Benjamin Davis (who was responsible for the tribute to Wright); and Ollie Harrington (whom poet Margaret Walker called Wright's 'last best friend'; whom Chester Himes called "the accepted leader for all the blacks of the Quarters... who single-handedly made the Café Tournon famous in the world"; and whom Julia Wright recalls as like a brother to her father). Of all the famed guests, the most impressive to me was Ollie Harrington, the famed cartoonist whom Langston Hughes declared America's greatest Black cartoonist and about whom my friend and former VCU colleague Tom Inge was at the time writing a book. I would see Ollie soon thereafter when he came to America for a tour of the two Harrington books Tom prepared. On the night before my departure, Paule, along with her son Evan, treated Joanne Gabbin and me to dinner and some night life in Paris.

I took the next picture that night of Joanne and Paule with blues singers Annette Lowman and Cynthia McPherson.

---

[19] Enthusiastic may be the preferred word choice, but I have consciously rejected it here.

The African Americans in Europe International Conference was attended by hundreds of scholars, writers, musicians, artists, actors, filmmakers, movie stars, and photographers from all over Europe, Africa, Asia, the US, Canada, and the Caribbean. I found myself bumping into acquaintances I had met almost everywhere I had ever traveled. I was constantly stopping to chat at conference sessions, at varied concerts and performances, at art and film exhibits, at restaurants, on the Métro, in elevators, in hallways, and on the streets. It was hard to even make my way through the hotel lobby because I had to stop to say hello to so many dear friends or to stare at some famous star or noted writer lost

JOANNE AND PAULE WITH BLUES SINGERS ANNETTE LOWMAN AND CYNTHIA MCPHERSON.

amidst crowds of adoring fans. It was in my hotel lobby that I joined my former University of California at Santa Barbara colleague Manthia Diawara and recent Nobel Laureate Wole Soyinka for a chat. I was, indeed, fortunate to be staying in the hotel that hosted most of the organizers and major stars of the conference, one that Conference coordinators Michel Fabre and Henry Louis Gates, Jr. had kindly recommended to me.

Under any circumstances, this fascinating conference in Paris would have been a memorable event for me, but thanks to the special extras that Paule arranged, it was a truly indescribable and unforgettable experience.

BARBARA GRIFFIN, PAULE, AND ME

On May 8, 1992, Paule and I had dinner with VCU Dean Elske Smith to celebrate the naming of the Elske Smith Lectureship, honoring the Dean, who, in a letter to me, noted that "It is fitting and pleasing that each of you [Paule and I] have been 'Lecturers'" (letter, April 3, 1992; I was the first recipient, on March 31, 1981, of the then-Arts and Sciences Lecturer Award). The three of us went out to dinner afterwards.

Paule joined our VCU colleagues at my retirement party from VCU, hosted by Bill and Barbara Griffin, shown here on May 2, 1992.

Coincidentally, at that party, Bill and VCU were bidding me adieu, and Bill's wife, Barbara, was welcoming me to the University of Richmond; Barbara was the chair of the UR English Department, where I would become The Jessie Ball DuPont Visiting Professor in September 1992.

I also joined the Ambassadors of ten African countries at VCU on May 26, 1992, for The Regional Economic Development Conference, a follow-up to the Williamsburg conference. I'm sure Paule was invited, and I believe she attended.

I introduced Paule when she spoke at UR in November 1992, my first guest lecturer after I moved to UR.

In the fall semester of 1993, I was excited to invite Paule to a Val Gray Ward performance at UR. News traveled of Val's appearance, and we had several famous visitors from further away. I expect we set a record at UR for the number of noted African American female writers gathered in our standing-room-only audience, including Sherley Anne Williams, Erna Brodber, Nikki Giovanni, Paule Marshall, Joanne Gabbin, and Karla Holloway, all of whom gathered at my home afterwards for a lively party.

PAULE AT CLA

In 1993 as VCU tried to fill Paule's position, I regularly consulted with the Chair, James Kinney, despite the fact that I was then working at UR.

On April 15, 1994, Paule again was the keynote speaker at the CLA Convention, this time at the Durham Omni hotel in Durham, NC. Her title was "Language Is the Only Homeland." She may be the only writer to have been invited to serve twice as banquet speaker at CLA. This was one of the few CLA banquets that I did not attend, but she gave me this picture from the conference.

In 1994 Paule wrote me from Kyoto to tell me she had talked with a Japanese professor who knows my work and she would get a copy of *New World Adams* from me to send him when she returned.

During a dinner on July 19, 1994, she told me about her trip to Japan, and then we went to a Marita Golden reading.

The next day, on July 20, 1994, she gave me a note with a gift of playing cards from Japan with illustrations "by one of the country's leading artists," apologizing for not remembering to bring it when we had dinner earlier: "Forgetfulness has become my middle name." She closed, "Enjoy them. They'll see to it you win each game."

That same day I wrote the following note to her: "Paule, I have such treasured items from some of your travels. I am grateful for your thoughtfulness. The cards[20] are beautiful—and you know that I shall get a lot of use from them. It was great to share your travels in Japan—especially over that scrumptious food. Thanks for a special evening. Capping it off with Golden's reading was the icing on the cake."

In 1994 Paule accepted an appointment as The Helen Gould Sheppard Chair of Literature and Culture at NYU. I was happy for her, but I feared that this would end our frequent get-togethers and her residency in Richmond.

Programme

TOASTMASTER
Burney J. Hollis
Chairman, Board of Directors
Morgan State University

GREETINGS

SILENT REFLECTION

POETRY READINGS
Ayesha J. Gallion
MAWK

A TOAST TO THE OCCASION

D I N N E R

PRESENTATION OF AWARD
Daryl C. Dance
University of Richmond

MAWA DISTINGUISHED WRITER AWARD
to
Paule Marshall, Novelist

KEYNOTE ADDRESS
Paule Marshall
Novelist

MUSICAL SELECTION
Delores Fleming-Jones

PRESENTATION OF SPECIAL AWARDS
Burney J. Hollis
Chairman of the Board of Directors
Louis H. Pratt
President

CLOSING REMARKS

MAWA BANQUET PROGRAM

---

[20] Playing cards. Paule knew that I am a bridge fanatic.

Fortunately, I was wrong on both trepidations.

On October 18, 1996, I introduced Paule and made the presentation to her when she received The MAWA Distinguished Writer Award and was the keynote speaker at the 17th Annual Conference Banquet of the Middle Atlantic Writers Association in Baltimore, MD.

On October 11, **1997,** I received a note to "Call Paule and plan trip to NY." She wanted us to plan some time together during my trip to New York in 1997 for the launching of *Honey, Hush!*

Paule proposed planning a book party for me at NYU, but I could not find the time with all of the events my publisher had planned. Nonetheless, after one full day of book launching events, Paule and I were able to enjoy a Broadway play, followed by dinner. It was fascinating to witness Paule in New York, where she immediately transformed into that charge-ahead, take-no-ransom New Yorker, barging through crowds and lines like her "juggernaut figure" M' Da-duh, in "To Da-duh, In Memoriam." It was all I could do to rush and try to follow closely in her wake as she wasted no time bolting through the crowds with a brusque "Sorry" if she jostled someone.

On July 11, 1999, I picked Paule up in Richmond at three for a lecture, following which we went out to dinner and discussed the possibility of my finding an agent. I don't recall how the subject came up. It may have been here that she gave me information to contact The Authors Guild in New York, a national group to which she belonged that advocated for writers. I did correspond with them, but this was after I had published my first book with W. W. Norton with what seemed to the Guild representative to be a good contract and a considerable advance. He said that they and most agents they might have recommended could not have secured for me any comparable deal. Thus ended my search for an agent.[21] However, Paule did

TAKEN AT MY BOOK SIGNING, WITH MY EDITOR AMY CHERRY, BEHIND, AND ONE OF MY CONTRIBUTORS, LISA JONES, SEATED LEFT OF ME

arrange for me to join her and her agent, Faith Child, for Faith's lecture and dinner on July 22, 1999.

On September 22, 2000, I spoke at the "Crossing Boundaries Conference" at NYU. Paule (who may have had something to do with my invitation, though she wasn't a part of the conference) made plans for us to get together during my trip to New York. In my calendar for September 23, 2000, I have the note, "Keep open for fun with Paule." She entertained me in her NYU apartment and joined us for the conference banquet.

On March 5, 2001, Paule and I attended a book signing with Merita Golden at 6:30 p.m. and, later, Golden's reading at VCU.

PAULE AT THE NYU CONFERENCE BANQUET

---

[21] I had through the years often talked to agents, but never had a promising offer from one.

On March 30, 2001, Paule read from *The Fisher King* at The VCU Visiting Writers Series in The Edward Temple Building; the program included a conversation with me and a book signing and reception.

On April 1, 2001, I picked Paule up at 6:50 p.m. for a 7 o'clock lecture, and then we went to a reception at Regenia Perry's.

On July 21, 2001, Paule and I went to the opening lecture of The David C. Driskell Collection of African American Art at the VMFA. We had a wonderful evening hearing the lecture, exploring the exhibition, and meeting and chatting with Driskell at another one of those exquisite receptions for which the VMFA is noted.

Another memorable event in 2001 was my taking Paule and a few other friends out to meet the renowned Katie Cannon, who had just accepted a position as The Annie Scales Rogers Professor of Christian Social Ethics at Union Presbyterian Seminary in Richmond. It was an unforgettable afternoon: we enjoyed a delicious lunch at Baker's Crust and remained for hours afterwards, enjoying the enlightening, enthusiastic, and often hilarious conversation.

The Virginia Commonwealth University
Visiting Writers Series presents

Paule Marshall

reading from her new novel
The Fisher King

Friday, March 30
7:00 pm

VCU T. Edward Temple Building, Room 1164, 1st Floor
901 West Main at Cherry Street

"Marshall's triumphant new novel reminds us why she is one of our premier African American voices."
— *Publishers Weekly*

Paule Marshall's *The Fisher King*, winner of the 2001 Award for Best Fiction from the Black Caucus of the American Library Association, is a moving and revelatory story of jazz, love, family conflict, and the artist's struggles in society, a novel that takes place on two continents and over five decades.

The author of two short story collections and four previous novels, including the now-classic *Brown Girl, Brownstones* and *Praisesong for the Widow*, Marshall is a 1992 recipient of a MacArthur Foundation "genius" Award.

The reading will be followed by a conversation with University of Richmond professor and author Daryl Cumber Dance, as well as a book signing and reception featuring music and refreshments. The event is free and open to the public. On-street parking is free and abundant.

For more information call 828-1329

One of our most delightful trips together was to the Langston Hughes Centennial Celebration at The University of Kansas (KU) in Lawrence, Kansas, February 7-11, 2002. Hughes was, as previously noted, one of Paule's favorite authors and literary mentors, and he was a great Paule Marshall advocate. Here we were in Hughes's hometown at a legendary celebration that, of course, featured Paule Marshall. I was not a guest speaker, but I was treated as such; and Paule and I were assigned to a delightful graduate student, Jeff Mack, who chauffeured, escorted, and hosted us at all events. Those events, featuring leading writers and scholars and memorable performances, were unforgettable, all planned and directed by the inimitable KU Professor Maryemma Graham and her colleagues. Paule, Jeff, and I had great times when it was just the three of us for a few quiet meals. He was a fantastic storyteller, often recounting tales of his beloved Sea-Island grandmother, whose influence on him he recounted in her Gullah language, modified enough to be sure we comprehended but accurate enough for us to appreciate its beautiful and colorful cadences and its distinctive grammar. As he related the influences of that powerful, remarkable, and devoted grandmother, I was reminded of Paule's adored M' Da-duh. Indeed, the three of us were all devotees of our powerful grands. I had been privileged to have mine live with me...... but I never shared my stories of her with Jeff and Paule. Like theirs, my grandmother regaled me with stories and songs; like theirs, my grandmother was the most prominent influence on my early life, my mentor, my friend, and my companion. But my grandmother was not the legendary folk figure that they had. Mine was down-home enough to prepare a few soul-food meals and occasionally let slip a phrase of Black English—but only for emphasis. My grandmother placed such a premium on fair complexion, straight hair, advanced education, "proper" speech, and her Harvard-educated husband that I decided not to share her with my companions at that time. I, too, treat—and celebrate—my grandmother in my writing, but I wasn't prepared to provide the necessary explanation and introduction at the conference honoring the poet who wrote off those on the "very high mountain" and always expressed his preference for "the so-called common element," adding, "and they are the majority—may the Lord be praised."[22]

When I came home, I shared anecdotes of the Hughes Conference with my daughter, Daryl Lynn, declaring that I wish she could have met Jeff. Surprisingly, a few years later, Daryl Lynn went to Kansas to be introduced to their graduate program, and who should be one of the students who hosted her?????

The very same Jeff Mack!

I was thus privileged to see—and enjoy the company of Jeff on scores of other trips to visit Daryl Lynn during her graduate studies at Kansas. I also saw him several years at CLA, where he became active for a while. I looked forward to sharing each meeting with Paule when I returned to Richmond, for we both often reminisced about our meeting with this remarkable young scholar.

During the spring of 2023, Jeff and I reminisced during a long telephone conversation about our time with Paule at the 2002 Hughes conference.

On May 22, **2004,** I picked up longtime Richmond friend Margaret Clay Crews and Paule to attend a program.

July 19, **2004,** I took Paule Marshall to dinner to thank her for contacts during and gifts from her Japan trip.

During 2004-05 I was delighted to have Paule share an occasional commentary about her plans for an upcoming visit to Harvard. Though Paule rarely expressed to me any passionate enthusiasm about her engagements, she was truly pleased to be planning to deliver a series of lectures on the theme of "Bodies of Water" at Harvard in 2005, lectures that became TR.

On August 3, 2006, I stopped for Paule at 5:45 p.m. for dinner at The Track Restaurant.

On July 25, 2007, I collected Paule for a ride to dinner.

In October 2007, I drove Paule to Baltimore, Maryland, for the festive 30th-anniversary celebration of *Callaloo*. See page 9 for a picture from that conference of Paule and me with Charles Rowell (founder and editor of *Callaloo)* and Joseph Skerrett (University of Massachusetts professor).

---

22 Hughes, "The Negro Artist and the Racial Mountain," in Henry Louis Gates, Jr., and Nellie Y. McKay, *The Norton Anthology of African American Literature.* New York: W. W. Norton, 2004. P.1312.

PAULE AND I WERE EARLY ARRIVANTS, ALONG WITH WILLIAM AND MARY PROFESSOR HERMINE PINSON, HER HUSBAND, DONALD PINSON, AND LUCILLE CLIFTON, FOR A READING AT THE *CALLALOO* EVENT

Also, particularly memorable for me through the years were those occasions when Paule's writer friends visited Richmond, and she invited me to their readings and then to a private dinner with them. Most notable among these were the visits of Louise Meriwether and Toni Cade Bambara. It was such a joy to see Paule with those very close friends. Her always big smile was even brighter. During Meriwether's visit (in 1995, I believe), I developed quite a friendship with her. After that visit, Meriwether sent me a copy of her latest book (*Fragments of the Ark*, 1994). We occasionally corresponded after that, and in 2020, I gratefully responded to Cheryl Hill's Go Fund Me request to help pay for the physical therapy that Meriwether needed after contracting and recovering from covid. The time spent with Toni Cade Bambara was unforgettable. She was every bit as funny as some of her hilarious writings.

Fragments of the Ark

Do Daryl,
How marvelous to see
you again on your own
turf with love,
Louise Meriwether
Feb '94

Of course, I included Paule when I had visitors during my years at UR, including Erna Brodber, Velma Pollard, Mervyn Morris, and Joanne Gabbin,[23] and some of those introductions also inspired relationships. For example, Pollard recently wrote to me:

Through you Paule took me to the mall one Saturday morning and bought me a clock, an atlas and a flashlight, I think. The first two are still in use. We kept in touch

---

[23] I can't recall whether she was in Richmond to join me when Walcott spoke at UR.

after Richmond. In fact somewhere around 2005 I gave a talk at NYU and she turned up rushing from a class. Then there was the annual Christmas card then nothing . . . (email 5/30/2022).

On April 2, 2008, I picked Paule up at 5:15 p.m. for a Lani Guinier lecture and reception at UR.

Despite Paule's occasional appearances at events at VCU and UR, so far as I know, she did not appear at The Virginia Museum of Fine Arts, The Library of Virginia, The Richmond Public Library, The Virginia Museum of History and Culture, the YMCA, or the YWCA, organizations that often feature local and international writers. Perhaps they did not invite her. Of course, if they invited her, she may have declined since Paule was very discriminating in the invitations she accepted and the time she took away from her writing.

Despite our long friendship and our continual interactions with each other, I don't remember giving Paule many gifts. Our main presents to each other were occasional books, books we wrote, or books from acquaintances and friends that one of us thought the other might like. I have previously mentioned her gifting me with an autographed reprint of *Soul Clap Hands and Sing*. I don't remember **any** gift I ever gave to Paule except books. I could never think of anything else that I might give her. The idea of selecting a piece of jewelry, an item of clothing, a household item, an art piece, a box of chocolates, or (God forbid!) a gift certificate for **Ms**. Paule Marshall was far beyond my imagination. I may have brought along flowers to some celebratory events, but I don't ever remember handing her any flowers, and I truly think that I might have found that awkward.

I keep thinking I must have found something appropriate for birthday and Christmas celebrations and for occasions where she was honored... but I don't recall anything.

Paule, on the other hand, did give me some special gifts from her travels, including the previously mentioned cards from Japan. One of my most cherished gifts is this framed Haitian folk painting that Paule brought to me after a trip to Haiti.

Paule kindly contributed to The Daryl Cumber Dance Endowed Travel Fund at Virginia State University upon its inception, and she contributed to The Veronica Bell Cumber Scholarship Fund at Elam Baptist Church.

Though tangible gifts from Paule Marshall were rare but memorable treasures, throughout our relationship, she blessed me with many even more prized "gifts." She frequently entertained me, regularly treated me to meals, and secured tickets for us to special events in Richmond and during our travels together.

Of course, the gift I treasured most during the years is the honor of her company, the magnanimity of her friendship.

Paule did not write many letters to me. She did send a number of gracious thank-you cards. And often, when she traveled, she would send me a card. I cherished those missives as much as she treasured hers from Langston Hughes.

From Vladimir, which was then within the USSR, she wrote on 2/9/89:

Московская улица.
Золотые ворота. Памятник архитектуры XII в.
Гостиница „Заря".
Мемориал в честь 30-летия Победы.
Скульптор В. Шанин
Архитектор Б. Шиганов
Фото Б. Мусихина

2/9/89

Air Mail

Dear Daryl — I'm sure I will be back in Richmond by the time you receive this, but I'm sending it anyway. What a rare, impressive country and people! I'm taking in as much as I can in my brief stay. See you soon. Paule

Куда Prof. Daryl Dance
c/o English Dept
VCU Box 2005
Richmond, VA 23284
Кому U.S.A.

Индекс предприятия связи и адрес отправителя

Индекс предприятия связи места назначения

The beautiful card has pictures of a Moscow Street, the 12th century Golden Arches, the Hotel "Sunrise," and a memorial erected to celebrate the 30th anniversary of the Soviet victory in 1945. The postmark is from Suzdal, a small town 16 miles north of Vladimir. Professor John Givens noted that "Both cities are part of the famous Golden Ring of ancient towns that encircle Moscow" and speculated that Paule bought the postcard in Vladimir and mailed it in Suzdal.[24]

---

[24] I was unable to confidently identify where Paule was when she wrote the card, and am grateful to Marcia Whitehead, Allen Dance, John Givens, Natalia Boykova, and David Brandenberger for providing the information above.

From Colorado (9/25/89), she sent a card:

It was a delight to imagine her unaccustomed sense of freedom and release as she set out to relax and celebrate her winning the MacArthur Award, traveling to Greece, from where she wrote me on August 8/9, 1992:

The cards themselves were things of beauty....

SOCIAL AND FAMILY EVENTS TOGETHER

As previously detailed, Paule and I frequently attended university and community programs, lectures, concerts, and dinners together, sharing almost equally in the planning. Paule would almost always plan a dinner along with any event to which she invited me. Clearly, our professional and social interactions overlapped. But Paule was also very much a part of my life apart from our university and professional relationship.

From her arrival in Richmond and her first few days at our home, Paule became and remained a part of my family, frequently joining us for holiday meals, general get-togethers, birthdays, weddings, and other celebrations, as well as, alas, my husband's wake.

I invited Paule to many of the social events in which Warren and I participated, including house parties. One of those most memorable to me was a rather large party we had at our home. As we were all sharing snacks and drinks and amiable conversations, Paule, who had driven herself that night, decided to leave for home: "...before it gets too late," she apologized. She bade adieu to all of the other guests.... Soon the doorbell rang. Paule had heard the catchy rhythms of one of the recordings Warren had just put on and the loud plaudits of the partygoers. She was frantically seeking to rejoin us, but we did not immediately hear the doorbell amidst the clamor as the party ratcheted up a few levels, so she was forced to thump on the door to get someone's attention. When she finally gained readmission, Paule rushed in, declaring with an exaggerated

PARTY JUNE 9, 1985

Jamaican accent, "Bob Marley call me back!" and joined us on the floor, singing with everyone, "We're jamming!"

This may well have been this party on June 9, 1985, which pictures Philmore and Margaret Howlette in the center and Connie Edwards, far right.

Recalling this night brings to mind what a music lover Paule was and reminds me that most, if not all, of the musical events we enjoyed together, were planned by Paule. Of the numerous events with Paule for which I have no specific dates and no pictures, one of the most memorable was a reggae concert at the Mosque. That is so unforgettable

because I had never before seen people dancing in the aisle of the orchestra seats in the Mosque—but here we were, Paule and I, dancing with other excited reggae fans—**in the aisle**—of the Richmond Mosque (now Altria Theater).

Paule joined Warren and me at the home of our dear friends William (Randy) and Wendy Johnson in May 1985 for another event;

The Johnsons were noted for their varied and frequent entertainments, and some of the events in their house are almost legendary among my friends. Wendy, a superb cook, would often prepare memorable treats—sometimes just for Warren and me. Then on other occasions, scores of people would be invited for special events, which included a lavish children's party every Christmas; a 4th of July lawn party to watch the fireworks (their house faced Dogwood Dell, the

HERE, PICTURED WITH RANDY, WENDY, AND WARREN. PAULE IS BESIDE WARREN, ALL BUT HER SMILING FACE COVERED BY OUR FRIEND MARGARET HOWLETTE.

Honored

Mrs. Esther Vassar of Fernleigh Drive entertained at home, May 10, for Dr. Daryl Dance who was recently promoted to full professorship at Virginia Commonwealth University.

Dr. Dance is the only black full professor in the School of Arts and Sciences.

Among those attending to congratulate Dr. Dance were Doctors and Mesdames W. R. Johnson, Frank Royal, Dennis Warner, Dr. Harry Royal, Attorney & Mrs. Oliver W. Hill, mother, Mrs. Veronica Cumber, Mr. & Mrs. Jerry Crews, Mrs. Martin Bloom, Dr. Dorothy Scura, and Paula Marshall.

Dr. Smith, Dean of the School of Arts & Sciences at VCU, Dr. Anne Zollar, Dr. Allen Barrett, Miss Denise Janka, Dr. Mable Wells, Linda McDonald, Dr. Daisy Reed, Theo Young, Head of Fashions and Designs at VCU, Dr. & Mrs. Paul Minton, Warren Dance husband of the honoree.

ESTHER VASSAR EVENT

site of fireworks in Richmond on the 4th and New Year's Eve); bridge gatherings; pool parties; and club celebrations (The Johnsons must have been in more than a score of civic, social, fraternal, and bridge clubs). For several years, a group of us would meet at the Johnsons on Christmas Eve for hors d'oeuvres, move on to the Carillon for the Nativity Pageant, then to the home of other friends for dinner, and to still another home of friends for desserts. The Johnsons were amenable to our bringing Paule to their home whenever she wished to join us.

Paule was one of those in attendance on May 10, 1985, when our VCU colleague, Ether Vassar, hosted a celebration of my promotion to full professor, making me the only black full professor in the School of Arts and Sciences, according to this newspaper article treating the event (the article with no identification is cut out of a newspaper, very likely The *Richmond Afro-American*).

Paule joined us another evening in 1985 when Warren and I celebrated Randy and Wendy's Anniversary at our home (probably June 1st or 2nd). Paule (with her back to the

camera) is seen in conversation that evening with Esther Vassar and Eunice Wilder.

In the next picture, she is in the forefront, seated with Henry (Skinny) Martin, Margaret Howlette, Carolyn Mosby, and Esther Vassar.

I'm not sure what the occasion was for this visit of VCU colleague Norrece Jones and Paule, but here the three of us are gathered around the Dance family room table in January 1988, holding up my just published *Folklore from Contemporary Jamaicans*). Perhaps they had dropped by to see my new book, pick up a copy, or just celebrate its publication with me.

Paule joined us for my son Warren's wedding to Tadelech (Taddy) on August 13, 1990, where she and our friend Esther Vassar were seated just behind my husband and me at the reception.

AERIAL VIEW OF THE RECEPTION - PAULE'S TABLE MARKED BY YELLOW CIRCLE

In a letter to Paule, dated November 5, 1992, I made the offer I made every holiday: "If you're in town for Thanksgiving, give me a call. Whatever we decide to do (eat in or out—do the whole turkey bit or some fast food if I'm lazy), we'd be happy to have you join us." I have no note or calendar entry to indicate whether or not Paule was with us that Thanksgiving.

On January 25, 1993, my calendar indicates "dinner with Paule," though I don't remember the place or details. I noted, too, that we scheduled a "Reading" afterwards.

PAULE AND WARREN ARRIVING AT ELAM WITH FLOWERS

HERE PAULE IS PICTURED WITH MY MOTHER. MY DEAR FRIENDS, DAVID AND CLARA HOGGARD, ARE JUST BEHIND MOTHER.

Paule rode with Warren and me to Elam Baptist Church[25] on December 19, 1993, to share in the announcement of The Veronica Bell Cumber Endowed Scholarship Fund, my family's birthday present to my mother (December 19th was the closest Sunday to my mother's December 23rd birthday).

[25] Daryl Lynn Dance and I have detailed the history of Elam Baptist Church in *The Lineage of Abraham: The Biography of a Free Black Family in Charles City, VA*, 2022. (Originally published in 1998).

I don't ever remember Paule going to our church in Richmond, though I'm sure I would have invited her. While she seemed very much at home at Elam, the fact is that I don't really know whether or not Paule was a churchgoer.

PAULE IS WITH THE PASTOR, REVEREND JAMES W. HAYES, AND WARREN. EVER THE HISTORIAN, PAULE APPRECIATED BEING IN ONE OF THE EARLIEST CHURCHES INDEPENDENTLY FOUNDED IN 1810 BY BLACKS.

For our 1993 Christmas dinner, she joined us along with her son Evan, announcing beforehand that "Evan will prepare the kir," her favorite drink, a cocktail of crème de cassis and champagne—and he came fully prepared. I don't recall whether I even offered our traditional eggnog (made with Charles City corn liquor, rum, bourbon, and brandy). She sent a note on the 27th:

Paule joined my family in Maryland for my son Allen's wedding on August 23,1997

PAULE AT WEDDING WITH JOANNE GABBIN, BARBARA GLENN (DEAN, SCHOOL OF HUMANITIES AND SOCIAL SCIENCES AT REYNOLDS), AND YOURS TRULY

Dec. 27, 1993

Dear Daryl—
Evan and I thank you for the wonderful visit chez les Dances on Xmas! It was every bit like being with family!
Enclosed is a brochure I promised Taddy I would send her.
A joyous and happy new year to all.
Paule

PAULE AND JOANNE ARE LOOKING UP AS I OFFER MY TOAST ON THE DECK OF ALLEN'S HOUSE.

Our colleague, Quincy Moore, a VCU colleague who had met Paule when he was a student at The University of Iowa, drove Paule to Maryland for the wedding. In a recent telephone conversation I had with him in July 2023, he recalled the delight of that drive with Paule.

On January 1, 1997, we had dinner together, according to a notation on my calendar. Perhaps she came to my house, or my family joined us at a restaurant.

On December 14, 1997, Paule joined me at the Barksdale Theatre for dinner and a play.

On December 15, 1997, I had lunch with Paule "to discuss a memorial contribution to Toni Cade Bambara."

My 60th birthday celebration was the biggest party at which Warren and I hosted her, beginning with drinks in the Rotunda Lobby at the bottom of the famed Grand Staircase, alleged at times to have been the staircase in *Gone with the Wind* and, at other times, to have inspired the staircase in that film. After dinner, we enjoyed dinner and dancing to the music of the Glenroy Bailey and Company Jazz Quartet in the beautiful ballroom of Richmond's only five-star hotel.

PAULE IS PICTURED HERE WITH ESTHER AND BRENNAN VASSAR AT MY 60TH BIRTHDAY PARTY ON JANUARY 17, 1998, AT THE JEFFERSON HOTEL.

On June 9, **1999,** I had lunch with Paule.

On April 9, **2000**—I hosted a **71st** birthday brunch for Paule at Tobacco Co with Esther Vassar, Virginia Union University Professor Evora Jones, Daryl Lynn, and Jackie McDonnough (my student and later colleague at VCU). The next day Paule wrote this wonderful note dated April 10, 2000:

I don't recall whether we went to the Marita Golden and Oliver Hill events that Paule mentioned in May, though Warren and I usually went to most Hill events, especially the annual Oliver White Hill Foundation event organized by Esther Vassar and the Oliver Hill Scholars events at UR.

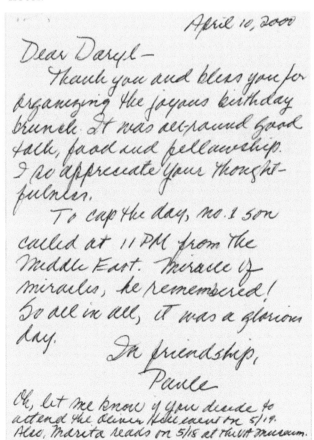

April 10, 2000

Dear Daryl—
Thank you and bless you for organizing the joyous birthday brunch. It was all-round good talk, food and fellowship. I so appreciate your thoughtfulness.
To cap the day, no. 1 son called at 11 PM from the Middle East. Miracle of miracles, he remembered! So all in all, it was a glorious day.
In friendship,
Paule
Oh, let me know if you decide to attend the Oliver Hill event on 5/19. Also, Marita reads on 5/18 at the VA museum.

PAULE (PICTURED HERE WITH DARYL LYNN) JOINED OUR FAMILY FOR THANKSGIVING DINNER AT THE TOBACCO COMPANY IN 2000

It may well have been that we took Paule to the affairs that she mentioned, but I don't have any note of it.

On January 25, 2001, I had dinner with Paule at 5:00 p.m. and an event with her at 7:00.

On September 9, 2001—Paule, eight others (including Katie Cannon and Velma Pollard), and I went to the VMFA. I don't recall further specifics about the evening.

Nov. 22, 2001, our family enjoyed Thanksgiving dinner with Paule at Tobacco Co.

On May 8, 2003, I picked Paule up for lunch.

Paule rarely refused an invitation to join me for trips to Charles City. She and my mother became great friends, and the historian in Paule relished our visits to Berkeley Plantation, Westover Plantation (where we were part of a celebration of Native Americans), and Indian Fields Restaurant, my mother's favorite. On April 22, 2005, I picked Paule up to take her and UR Visiting Scholar, Kansas poet Denise Low, to visit the Chickahominy Indian Reservation and the Samaria Indian Church in Charles City, to visit the site of the early arrivals of Europeans on the shores of the Chickahominy River, and to have lunch at Indian Fields Restaurant. Our tour was coordinated by my cousin Richard M. Bowman, the noted expert on Charles City History. Any excursion with Richard was an engrossing and informative one, and Richard enjoyed the exchanges with these two enthusiastic scholars. In 2019 The Richard M. Bowman Center for Local History was erected on the Charles City Court House Grounds.[26]

On May 19, **2005,** I picked Paule up at 5:50 p.m. to have dinner at the Track Restaurant across from the Byrd Theatre in Richmond.

Photo to the right is Paule joining us at my son Allen's house in July 2005 for our Bon Voyage party for Daryl Lynn, who was leaving to begin her graduate studies at The University of Kansas.

PAULE AND I ARE SURVEYING THE SERVING ISLAND.

---

[26] Richard Bowman died on October 30, 2014.

PAULE WITH MY GRANDDAUGHTER, VERONICA, AND MY FRIENDS JACKIE THOMAS AND
DELORES ROBINSON.

In August 2008, my children invited Paule to a surprise 50th Anniversary lunch for Warren and me at Maggiano's Little Italy Restaurant in Short Pump.

PAULE AT OUR FAMILY TABLE WITH OUR GRANDDAUGHTER; PAULE IS CHATTING WITH MARGARET CREWS.

PAULE AND OUR FRIEND, BOBBY GILBERT.

It was a beautiful and joyous event with our three children, both grands, and several longtime friends. I'm not sure how Paule got to the event, but Warren or I took her home afterwards.

On April 9, 2009, I joined one of Paule's friends who planned a dinner to celebrate Paule's 80th birthday at Rowlands, 2131 W. Main Street, in Richmond.

On April 14, 2011, Paule and I went out for dinner at 5, and then we went to see "Things Fall Apart" at UR's Jepson Theatre.

During several of Paule's Richmond years, Warren and I were members of the Bull and Bear Private Club atop One James Center in Downtown Richmond. Paule occasionally shared a meal with us there. We usually began with drinks and appetizers in the Lounge Bar, with the ever-attentive bartenders managing a kir to her liking. We then moved on to the dining area, where I always reserved the table at the Northwest Corner, with its amazing and unmatched 21st-floor views of the city and The James River. We all looked forward to Chef Michael Hall's acclaimed French-inspired Southern Soul-food cuisine. In its Glory Days, The Bull and Bear had no peers among Richmond restaurants for stunning ambiance, great drinks, splendid service, and gourmet delights. The Club has since closed, and Chef Hall has moved on to a series of other ventures: The Berkeley, M. Bistro, Spoonbread Bistro, Spoonbread Deux, Black Market Dining, and The Chef's Table. I continue to enthusiastically follow him wherever he offers his legendary fare.

There are numerous other social events for which I don't recall nor have notes of either time, place, or occasion.

PAULE AND SOME OTHER FRIENDS, INCLUDING MY NEIGHBOR, DELORES ROBINSON

This next picture is of a party that Paule hosted at her condo, the only one I recall attending.

WARREN IS THE THIRD PERSON FROM THE LEFT.

Paule, along with some mutual Caribbean friends, attended the wake for my husband on Friday, September 2, 2011. I don't remember seeing her at the funeral, the burial, or the ensuing reception. However, because of the trauma of the occasion and the large number of friends in attendance, my recollection of all of the events of Warren's passing and burial is something of a maze.

On Feb. 12, 2012, I stopped for Paule **at** 3:15 p.m. for a movie at the Bow Tie Theatre. We likely did dinner afterwards. This was probably the first time we got together after my husband's death.

While throughout her Richmond years, Paule joined Warren and me at numerous social events, met a number of our acquaintances, and came to be quite fond of a few of our friends, I don't think Black Richmond Society very often reached out to her. As far as I know, none of the dominant Black women's organizations (such as The Links, The Society, The Girl Friends, The Chums, The Epicureans, and the Greek Sororities) sent her invitations to social events or even queries about headlining some of their programs. Paule was certainly not one to be attracted to or seek association with "The Black Elite" (sometimes referred to as "Black Bourgeoisie," or "Our Kind of People," or the Black FFVs, or those she describes in *The Fisher King* as "stuck-up, show-off, siddity" [68]); and she may not have responded had there been any overtures.

Paule was, however, enthusiastically embraced by the Caribbean community in Richmond. I often drove Paule to special events sponsored by the Association of Jamaicans in Richmond (AJM), especially their Jamaican Independence Day Celebration and Family Memorial Day picnic. Most of the years that Paule was in Richmond during the Christmas holiday, we both attended the legendary annual Christmas party sponsored by Trinidadians Kaestner and Jacqueline (Jackie) McDonnough. Jackie had been my student and later became our colleague at VCU. We also attended together several events of the AJM at the home of William and Beryl Riley.

In preparation of this memoir, I asked some of our mutual Caribbean friends if they had any pictures of Paule, but they couldn't find any. One said that the problem was that "Paule was so reticent, so retiring that she stayed in the background." He noted that he had several pictures of her with her back to the camera or hardly visible in the background as he was taking pictures of others.

The Waning Years

As time passed following Warren's death, my retirement from the University of Richmond, Paule's retirement from NYU, my year as The Sterling A. Brown Chair at Howard, and my belated discovery of a sister in 2012,[27] I saw less and less of Paule and had fewer and fewer calls. The last time I remember picking her up was when I took her and my elderly cousin Olivia (Libby) Slade McGill to a movie. We enjoyed the movie but somehow were separated afterwards. After finally reuniting and getting to my car, both Paule and Libby were too exhausted to stop at a restaurant for the dinner I had also planned. Instead, I dropped them both off in front of their condos and, as always, waited until they went in their doors. I don't remember the date, but it was probably in 2012 or 2013.

During the next three years, friends and associates constantly asked me about her, our former Dean writing, "Do you see much of Paule Marshall? How is she doing? Do tell her hello from me if/when you see her" (email, December 19, 2013). I responded, "I've called Paule twice in the last two weeks with no response. I expect she may be in Europe with her son and two grandchildren. She was doing well when last I saw her" (email, 12/20/2013). Similar correspondences with our friends and colleagues continued, and I became more and more concerned as years passed, and the phone calls became rarer and rarer....

And then I did not hear from her at all.........

Finally, I traced Evan down and wrote to him on January 5, 1916, "For over a year now, I have not been able to reach Paule. Her Richmond number rings, but no answer. Please let me know where your mom is and how she is." Evan immediately responded, noting that she was home and had one carekeeper. He had tried to hire a second, but she "rejected her out of hand and basically told [her] to leave her apartment forthwith" (email, 1/5/2016). I smiled as I pictured that scene, but my eyes teared a bit too. I could imagine that the idea of a caretaker must have been offensive to my independent friend. Just having someone else hanging around her private quarters would certainly be viewed as an unwelcome encroachment.

Evan instructed me to call at a specified time when the caretaker was there and explain to her who I was, but he warned that Paule would not engage in a lengthy conversation for fear that she might reveal that her mind was not what it used to be. I immediately followed his directions, made the call, and asked to speak to Paule. After a long lapse, she came to the phone. We spoke for a brief while—and that was usually the case for us—neither of us had ever been one for prolonged telephone chats. The sad difference of this call was that we were making no plans for a future lecture, concert, meal, or even a walk. There was no talk about our children and grands. I slowly and sorrowfully put the handset on the cradle.

The painful recognition that my friend was experiencing some of the symptoms of senescence called to mind her frequent detailed (one might even say obsessive) exploration of the aging of her characters, such as forty-year-old Merle in *The Chosen Place, The Timeless People*:

> She was no longer young. Her body had already begun the slow, irreversible decline toward middle age. The flesh that had once been firm was beginning to slacken and lose hold. Under the bodice of her dress there was the slight weary telltale droop to her small breasts . . . (4)

Then there are Avey Johnson and her sexagenarian and septuagenarian friends in *Praisesong for the Widow*. Paule carefully details the physical, mental, and emotional aspects of aging through these and scores

---

[27] I write about this discovery and our meeting in *Here Am I*, 88-117.

of other men and women in almost every one of her novels. Indeed, *Soul Clap Hands and Sing* is a collection of tales about old men, having as its epigraph W.B. Yeats's "Sailing to Byzantium."

An aged man is but a paltry thing,

A tattered coat upon a stick, unless

Soul clap its hands and sing.

Aging is a critical part of almost all of her stories, but it is noteworthy that with the octogenarians, nonagenarians, and centenarians, the emphasis on the distortion of old age is balanced by the greater focus on their dignity and power.

Representative is Avey's spiritual guide in *Praisesong*, Lebert Joseph, "a stoop-shouldered old man with one leg shorter than the other" (160):

He was close to ninety perhaps, his eyes as shadowed as the light in the rum shop and the lines etched over his face like the scarification marks of a thousand tribes. His slight winnowed frame scarcely seemed able to support the clothes he had on. Yet he had crossed the room just now with a forced vigor that denied both his age and infirmity. And his hands, large, tough-skinned, sinewy, looked powerful enough to pick up Avey Johnson . . . and deposit her outside.

(*Praisesong* 161)

And then there is her favorite ancient, Da-duh:

The details of her slight body and of the struggle taking place within it were clear enough—an intense, unrelenting struggle between her back which was beginning to bend ever so slightly under the weight of her eighty-odd years and the rest of her which sought to deny those years and hold that back straight. . . . [her] face . . . was as stark and fleshless as a death mask, that face. The maggots might have already done their work, leaving only the framework of bone beneath the ruined skin and deep wells at the temple and jaw. But her eyes were alive, unnervingly so for one so old.

("To Da-duh, In Memoriam," 96-97)

Aging was a stage Paule had given a lot of thought to, studied, analyzed, portrayed, and helped generations of readers to understand. Though I did not see much of her during her waning years, I am sure she, too, was gracefully denying those years and "hold[ing her] back straight."

....

Evan informed me of his plans to return to Richmond on January 18, 2017, to make arrangements for moving his mother to an independent living facility. I offered whatever help I could provide, and we agreed we would get together during his trip. He later informed me that the bad weather during his visit prevented the planned trips to look at senior facilities.

In 2018 a mutual friend informed me that she had seen Paule at Imperial Plaza, an assisted living facility in Richmond. She had spoken to her, but Paule did not remember her. Our friend was pained to witness the confused and lonely figure sitting apart from others in the room where the senior citizens were gathered.

She cautioned me not to visit.

Then, in 2019, I was in touch with Evan and University of Maryland Professor Mary Helen Washington (hereafter, MHW) as they began planning a biography of Paule. Evan was Paule's only son, her sole heir, and she had given him power of attorney over her business affairs. He gave Washington sole access (until her book is finished) to all of Paule's papers in her possession and in his own, accompanied her to interview his mother, and provided several interviews himself. Both MHW and Evan sought some information from me. I gave Mary Helen an interview, provided her a detailed list of Marshall's activities in Richmond, and lent her a number of pictures. Evan asked me to identify some people in a picture with Paule and me. Among others, I identified Regenia Perry, and he asked me to give his regards to her, adding, "I still have fond memories visiting with her in Richmond as Hampton college students" (email, April 7, 2020). When I passed on the message to Regenia, she was delighted to hear from him and remembered that of all the students who stayed with her, Evan was the only one who sent a thank-you note.

Paule would have been pleased.

It's amazing how paths cross and what impressions remain for 30+ years.

On February 4, 2019, MHW wrote to me as she and Evan began scrutinizing Paule's papers:

I've been seeing your name and face a lot—among Paule's papers. When I visited Paule a few months ago, her son Evan asked me about doing her biography, and though I am hesitant to undertake such a journey, I began to work on it without actually realizing what I was getting myself into. Seeing your picture made me realize how close you are to Paule, and I'm wondering if I can talk this over with you.

I eagerly agreed to talk with her and welcomed her to stay with me when she was working in Richmond. On Feb. 21, 2019, I sent MHW directions to get to my house, where she spent the night as she interviewed Paule and Evan the next couple of days. She also interviewed me and returned for a second time to continue her research in Richmond. I gathered pictures that I had of Paule and loaned them to her.

. . . .

(I expect that process of assembling those pictures for MHW may have been an unrecognized, at the time, stimulus for this memoir)

. . . .

My correspondence with MHW continued. On March 1, 2019, she wrote to me:

I would like your notes. We can talk about them as part of another interview. It was so lovely staying with you—your house is comfy, beautiful, and easy to get used to. I absolutely adored your soup. I marvel at your gracious hospitality and hope to imitate it.[28] A big hug and thanks for taking me in.

. . . .

And then the sad news came of Paule's passing on August 12, 2019, something that I am still processing.

I am hoping my work on this photo-memoir, my celebration of our friendship, will bring . . . . .

What? . . . .

Perhaps assuagement, some relief, some release, some cheer, some answers to the questions, some filling of the void. There is some consolation in the fact that Paule's remarkable oeuvre assures that she will never

---

[28] She did later invite me to an event at The University of Maryland, College Park, but I was unable to attend.

die. My admiration for her began long before I ever saw her, and my appreciation of her brilliant work will never fade. In fact, as I have reread a number of her works since her death (many of them for the fifth or sixth time), I am even more amazed at her talent—her remarkable characterization (she created memorable characters of every age, every race, every nationality, every class, every gender and sexual orientation); her astonishing rendering of place (which includes varied views of nations, landscapes, houses, bars, churches, mountains, seas, beaches, trees, flowers, roads, animals, insects, cars, carts, temperatures, smells); her precise and unmatched articulation of dialogue; and her knowledge of history, of politics, of psychology, of religion, of the arts—particularly the variety of forms of Afro-based music, everything from spirituals, gospel, blues, and calypso to reggae and jazz. There are scores of examples, but two must be mentioned: *The Fisher King* is one of our outstanding jazz novels, and "Brazil" (in *Soul Clap Hands and Sing*) is basically a samba piece, both having intricate descriptions of performances that transport you to experiencing a live show, and both are to some degree framed by music.

Paule's splendid oeuvre will not allow me to lament her passing.

To lose myself in a rereading of one of her stories evokes the delight and the amazement that always inspired me to regard her as a bigger-than-life luminary.

. . . .

Upon notice of her demise, the Wintergreen women and other associates immediately shared their grief with me. Joanne Gabbin wrote:

Her radiant smile, her wonderful ability to capture the "big-mouth" wit of the island women she admired, her tenacious dedication in honoring her Bajan roots come to mind when I think of her.... May she rest in the peace and beauty of the turquoise sea and red bougainvillea of her beloved Barbados. (email August 15, 2019)

In her note to me, Maryemma Graham recalled being introduced to Paule by George Lamming when she was in grad school and told me that she was preparing to teach a "'forms' course in the spring.... My 'form' will be autobiography, but I like the idea of using *Brown Girl, Brown Stones* because of its autobiographical arc and all the border crossings I can do both in terms of genre and place." (email August 29, 2019).

Another Kansas friend, Giselle Anatol, shared with me a beautiful tribute that I forwarded to Evan. It ended:

Rest in peace, Ms. Marshall. You will be sorely missed, but we will continue to share your words and art. They have the kind of power that lured a young girl like me away from an early determination to become a physician. From you, I learned that I could make a difference in the world with a pen as well as a scalpel <u>or</u> a sword.[29]

Several friends and former students wrote to express their sympathy to me. Typical was Pianapue Early's email on 8/17/2019, "I hope God is still taking care of you. I read of Paule Marshall's death and wanted to express my sympathy. I remember you and Dr. Marshall were colleagues, and we read some of her works."

Paule's death was noted in several international publications. Major American papers, including the *NY Times* and the *Washington Post*, had headline stories on August 16, 2019, providing glowing accounts of her career and her influence. The *Richmond Times Dispatch* (August 16, 2019), the *VCU News* (August 16, 2019),

---

[29] "Remembering Paule Marshall." *The Project on Black Writing.* September 3, 2019.

and the *Richmond Free Press* (August 23, 2019) offered lengthy articles on the passing of the famous writer who had spent much of her last thirty-five years here in Richmond. In addition to noting her significant writing career, they also gave her credit for, in the words of the *VCU News*, bringing "eminent black writers to our campus, including Toni Morrison and James Baldwin, writers who were her friends."

Marshall did, in fact, bring numerous eminent writers to VCU, writers who were her friends, but I don't recall that they included Toni Morrison and James Baldwin. I brought James Baldwin to VCU in 1978—before Paule came to VCU; the only other visit that I recall of James Baldwin to Richmond was when he came for the opening of his *The Amen Corner* with Bea Bush in 1976. The only time I remember Toni Morrison at VCU was when she spoke at the Siegel Center on October 2, 2002, as part of a program sponsored by VCU and UR that occurred on October 2-3, 2002, long after Paule had retired from VCU—I don't recall that Paule was there for either of those readings.

On August 29, 2019, Evan informed me that he "was so fortunate to be by my mother's side the afternoon she peacefully took her last breath and departed this life" (email). He added that he would inform me regarding his plans for a memorial for Paule, which was currently on hold because of the Covid Pandemic. I sent my condolences and let him know I would look forward to hearing more as his plans developed.

On April 7, 2020, Evan informed me that he had received scans of the material in his mother's safe deposit box, "which turns out to be a treasure trove of documents, letters, and photographs." I was elated to hear that so much of her important archival material was preserved and would soon be available.

On October 26, 2020, MHW wrote to ask if she could spend the night on a trip to Richmond to get something from Paule's storage place. I regretfully responded on the same day, "It would be wonderful to see you, but I am in isolation and not having visitors at all. As soon as this pandemic passes, you will be welcomed whenever you are in Richmond." I was disappointed at the loss of the opportunity to catch up with MHW's project and enjoy some company—one of the many frustrations caused by this darn pandemic. However, as much as I always enjoyed MHW's company, I was isolating and had had no visitors for over two years, not even my children who would have traveled here on public transportation. I received my local children occasionally on the front porch, properly distanced and masked.

On May 5, 2022, MHW wrote to ask for help in finding "Virginia," a figure in TR whom Paule describes as a white-looking fellow "travelin' woman" (39) who had been her friend since she moved to Richmond, an octogenarian in September 1998 (at which time Paule would have been 79). I had no idea who she was, so I asked a few mutual friends if they remembered anyone fitting that description. They did not. I could only suggest to MHW that she try Norrece Jones, our former VCU colleague.[30]

I had, in fact, been wondering who "Virginia" was ever since I first picked up TR. She certainly didn't fully fit the description of any of Paule's Richmond friends that I had ever met or of any Richmonder I knew. I could not help but reflect on the many times I had talked with Paule about the autobiographical nature of some of her characters. She told me in our interview, "My characters... are sometimes drawn from life but transformed to suit my fictional purposes; usually, though, they're pure inventions."[31] Admitting on one occasion in my interview with her that *Daughters* was her "most personal novel," she added, "I hasten to add that the personal and the autobiographical have been transformed, disguised, reinvented." Finally, I

---

[30] I next heard from MHW in April 2023, when she informed me that she would soon be returning to Richmond to consult Paule's papers again.

remember her telling me that she needed Viney in *Daughters* to represent certain experiences, and thus, she continued:

> In creating a personal history for Viney, I decided to put one such battlefield[32] across the road from her family's house in Petersburg. The house is also put a few doors down from their church, The Triumphant Baptist (and there is a Triumphant Baptist Church in Richmond--that's where I got the name). Viney's Triumphant Baptist Church also faces the battlefield. And I just let that configuration of battlefield, church and her family's house make their statement about an entire history.

It is clear that Paule, given her fascination with AA history and her goals in this story, needed a Virginia, a representation of US history with its slavery, plantations, miscegenation, Civil War reenactments, and statues, as well as its African American FFVs (First Families of Virginia). Paule's Virginia was, like her, an international traveler and a widow. Virginia had traveled all over the world with her husband, an artist, and a cultural attaché. One of her grandfathers was one of the wealthiest of the White FFVs (the source of Virginia's color), and another was once a chattel laborer and then a sharecropper. That Virginia's name in TR is thematic is consistent with Paule's naming elsewhere, as, for example, in *Daughters*, where the names reinforce Paule's theme of a constellation, with the PM being the polestar around which Estelle (Stellar), Astral, Ursa, and Celestine (celestial) gravitated. Here the theme was African Diasporan history. And Virginia—the Virginia that Paule created—filled every aspect of the bill.

In TR, Paule walks along the James River with Virginia and tells her about her trip to Paris to the African Americans in Europe Conference. Paule also recounts her travels through the countryside of Barbados, where she watches the last bit of sun vanish below the sea in Grenada. She reflects on the arrival of Africans at Port Comfort, the slave auction blocks in Richmond, and the plantations up and down the James River. Many rivers and many roads meet in her Virginia character—and in the novelist herself, roads that reflect the focus throughout Paule's magnum opus of Africans in Africa, Africans in the United States, and Africans in the Caribbean. Here their confluence is in Virginia.

THE JAMES RIVER IN RICHMOND, VA, PHOTO BY ALLEN C. DANCE

---

[32] She was referring to Civil War battlefields.

Perhaps, I decided... perhaps Virginia was what Paule said most of her characters were: something of "the personal and the autobiographical... transformed, disguised, reinvented" but ultimately "pure invention" (interview).

Scholars and friends will, for many years, continue to wrestle with the magnificent opus of my dear friend. They—and I—will continue to seek answers.

In the meantime, many continue to seek answers from me. One noted Caribbeanist, a bit concerned when she heard MHW say that she had all of Paule's papers, wrote:

> How come the university did not acquire them? Her son it seems gave them to her. But they should be placed somewhere as archive. Can you follow up on that. Some of these kids do not know. (email 3/27/2020)

I did follow through, writing for information to her son, Evan Marshall, and her biographer, MHW. Evan wrote me on March 31, 2020, that Paule donated the majority of her papers to Brooklyn College when she retired from NYU; and that he was considering Schomburg as a possible place for the materials that MHW still has until she completes the biography. MHW wrote me on April 3, 2020, apprising me that Evan "has not decided where her papers will be held."

I shared the information with the concerned scholar, who wrote back, "Can you tell Evan that it has to go into a secure archive after MHW finishes with them. Sometimes the children don't realize this is valuable material they have" (email 3/29/2020).

MHW continued to contact me as she finished up her biography on Paule. On May 12, 2023, she wrote to tell me she was coming to Richmond on May 23 to do more work in Paule's storage facility, and she would like to talk further with me about my interview with Paule. We arranged that she would stay with me and we could have our dialogue. However, she contacted me on May 23, devastated at the news that all of Paule's papers had been "cleared out" of the storage unit. Though I was relieved that MHW had many of the principal Marshall papers safe in her possession, the loss of all the rest of the papers, some of them "very important things" (MHW's email), left me feeling painfully distressed. I could not sleep for several nights, thinking of what could/should/might have been done to avoid this catastrophe and remembering the "concerned scholar's" earlier prophetic advice. MHW's call a few days later offered some release. We bewailed the grievous and incomprehensible loss. Nonetheless, we had a good interview, and we also enjoyed bringing each other up to date on the progress of our current Marshall projects.

But... the loss of Paule's valuable papers still haunts me. Almost every night, I conjure up some restoration of them: Sometimes MHW just misunderstood, and the papers are still safely stored in Paule's storage unit. Sometimes the trash collector, suspecting that these papers are special, just takes them home and sticks them in his attic. Sometimes the papers are being thrown into a fire at the storage facility when someone snatches them out of the flames and archives them, their burnt edges forever testifying to their lucky rescue (as was the case with Zora Neale Hurston's papers). Sometimes the owners of the storage facility recognize their worth and, instead of actually throwing them away, sell them on the black market. Sometimes, with no explanation, the papers somehow turn up at a yard sale. Sometimes the family just makes up the story of their disappearance while holding on to them until their value increases.

Of course, I'm always the heroine who finally discovers the lost treasure.

AFTERWORD

Paule's death caused me to reflect anew on her move to Richmond, which had been and still remains a surprise to me. I was, at first, shocked that this die-hard New Yorker actually accepted a two-year visiting appointment with us at VCU, not exactly in league with the prestigious universities with which she had formerly been associated (Yale, Columbia, U of California at Berkeley, Iowa Writers Workshop). I was later surprised to read in TR Paule's admission, "I needed a job, though, at the time" (41). It had simply not occurred to **me** at that time that she **needed** a job. She certainly didn't seem to lack offers of visiting appointments from prominent universities, and she always seemed to be an efficient money manager as a writer who was determined to maintain time for her craft. Then, I was further shocked that she later accepted the offer of a tenured professorship at VCU, committing herself to teaching one semester of each school year. However, later I learned that she was, indeed, **pleased** to take what she called in TR "my first real job" (41).

Perhaps, this may have been a period in her life where a regular salary and the guarantee of tenure offered her some needed assurance, insurance.

Then when she went to NYU after her retirement from VCU, I was certain that she would never return to Richmond. It was clear when I visited her that she truly loved her NYU apartment. She clearly enjoyed being back in New York with its subways, its Broadway plays, and its mix of varied cultures and languages. Paule was first and foremost a New Yorker; her second love was the Caribbean; and perhaps her third was Paris. Richmond was alien land, the heart of the Confederacy, reminders of which provoked nightmares in the newly-arrived Paule. The sudden appearance in downtown Richmond of "men in dress uniform gray, swords at their sides" evokes fear in Paule:

> I'm suddenly chattel cargo, merchandise, goods, a commodity to be bought and sold in the Bottom. (TR 51).

Just as suddenly, Paule realizes that what she is witnessing is a reenactment, "perhaps the South's most enduring ritual." (TR 52)

Throughout her time in Richmond, Paule regularly traversed Monument Avenue, one of the most beautiful streets in the nation, a cobblestone street of stately homes with tree lined media in the center. Until 2020 imposing confederate memorials dotted the avenue, one of the most grandiose of which was the Robert E. Lee statue at a traffic circle on Monument and Allen Avenues, a few blocks west of VCU and a couple of blocks north of her home. Clearly Monument Avenue was another reminder of the slaveholding South that provoked Paule's nightmares. She did not live to see the 2020 protests against the

PHOTO COMPLIMENTS OF ALLEN CUMBER DANCE.

monuments that led to the symbolic attacks with graffiti and then their removal in 2021.

I always realized that the slow pulse of life in Richmond couldn't compare with New York and Paris, and Virginia certainly lacked the tropical climate and the clear blue sea of the Caribbean. But once Paule purchased her condo at 503 S. Davis Avenue, #6, she held on to it.

PAULE'S CONDO

Even when she was at NYU, she returned frequently to spend time at the Richmond condo. Perhaps the explanation had been offered to me when I interviewed her on June 14, 1991:

So it's taken a while to adjust to some of those things [the Confederate monuments and the reenactments]. Generally, though, living in Richmond these seven years has been a positive experience. It's slowed me down some, and after having lived in New York City all my life, I needed to decelerate. It's also provided me with the opportunity--because I find life here less pressured--to work on my inner being, so to speak, and to unburden myself of a lot of past negative programming. So I've become a sort of happier, more relaxed and younger person even as I become a Gray Panther. [Laughter] And Richmond has also proven to be a good place for me to get the writing done.

And "get the writing done," she did! In Richmond, she completed the three major works that capped her remarkable publishing career: *Daughters*, *The Fisher King*, and *Triangular Road*.

Nonetheless, so worried did I continue to be about Paule's adjustment to Richmond that it is only now, in retrospect, that I am seeing how clear it was that there were some attractions of her condo that had a lasting appeal to her: the three lakes in the area, with a view of Swan Lake from her condo;

its location in Byrd Park with its wonderful walking trails; its proximity to The Robins Nature Center and to Dogwood Dell with its amphitheater and Ha'Penny Stage, its annual Festival of the Arts, its Fourth of July Fireworks, its Nativity Pageant on Christmas Eve, its special performances and concerts, which we sometimes sat on the lawn to watch. Occasionally we did the mile-long trail in Byrd Park, me trying to keep up with the speed walker. After a while, she would announce, "I'll wait for you at the lake," and off she would dash. Gratefully, I returned to my comfortable pace. We met at the lake, and the conversation continued. When my seven-year-old grandson visited Richmond after a few years in Singapore, Paule directed me, "You must bring Master **Yoseph**" [it was a delight to hear Paule's emphasis on names she liked, and Yoseph's was one of them] for a walk around the lake. "He'll enjoy waving at the folks in the paddle boats and feeding the ducks." When I arrived with Yoseph, she was waiting with bottled water and something for him to feed the ducks. She loved her location within walking distance of VCU, the Mosque Theater, the Fan District, and Carytown (with its quirky neighborhood, unique boutiques, Byrd Theatre [the oldest in Richmond], and great restaurants). Just as, during the early years of her career, she escaped New York to write in Barbados and Grenada, she later settled on Richmond as an escape destination.

There was a certain consolation that I finally reached after all of these years of worrying that the move I initiated might not have been fulfilling for my idol... that I might have been selfishly motivated by a desire to boast so famous a writer as my colleague. Or that I coveted for VCU the prestige of universities with writers in residence (like Faulkner at UVA; Morrison at SUNY and Rutgers; Giovanni at VA TECH; and Angelou at Wake Forest). It took me all these years to realize that, ultimately, my efforts were also critically rewarding for Paule. Like many of the characters she created who were seeking their home, their place, their identity, she, too, finally found **her** home. Not the place she expected, but a place in the American South where her triangular roads met, and the circle was closed. Paule even took the unusual step (for her!) of having stationery printed with her Richmond address.

Paule B. Marshall
503 South Davis Ave. #6
Richmond, VA 23220-5757

There is now, I see, every reason to conclude that perhaps here in the dreaded South, she, like another New Yorker she created (Avey), "felt centered and sustained... restored to her proper axis" (*Praisesong* 254).

And so it was that in this unlikely capital of the Confederacy where I had directed her path, she "peacefully took her last breath and departed this life"[33]— joining the ancestors whose memory she so frequently evoked.

I am proud... proud that Richmond became the *Chosen Place* of this *Brown Girl*. Let all the *Daughters Clap Hands and Sing* a *Praisesong* that her *Triangular Road* led my esteemed colleague, my favorite novelist, my dear friend here—to "The River City" in the state "for lovers."[34] The sub-title of the second chapter in TR is "I've Known Rivers: The James River." This title clearly is reminiscent of Langston Hughes' famous early poem, "The Negro Speaks of Rivers," with its refrain," I've Known Rivers," a celebration of the strength of Black heritage and perseverance garnered through the many rivers through which he and our ancestors have passed.

---

[33] This quotation is from Evan's description of her death to me.
[34] Richmond is often dubbed "The River City" and Virginia has since 1969 boasted the now world-famous slogan "Virginia Is for Lovers."

SUNSET - THE JAMES RIVER IN RICHMOND, VA. PHOTO BY ALLEN CUMBER DANCE

In closing, I dare to hope that I have managed in this little memoir what my ever-prescient friend Joanne Gabbin promised when she wrote to me on August 28, 2019, when I was unable to provide her a tribute to Paule:

Please don't worry about it. When it is time, you will give her a fitting tribute.

It seems fitting to close my tribute to Paule, "my treasured elder friend,"[35] with the same Hughes poem she chose to end her "Homage to Mr. Hughes":

I loved my friend.
[She] went away from me
There's nothing more to say.
The poem ends,
Soft as it began--
I loved my friend.
(Langston Hughes, *The Weary Blues*)

---

[35] I borrow Paule's description of Hughes (TR 33).

Works Cited

By Daryl Cumber Dance:

- "African American Literature by Writers of Caribbean Descent." *The Cambridge History of African American Literature.* Ed. Maryemma Graham and Jerry W. Ward, Jr. Cambridge: Cambridge University Press, 2011. Paperback, 2015. 377-404.
- *Fifty Caribbean Writers: A Bio-Bibliographical and Critical Sourcebook.* Westport, Connecticut: Greenwood Press, 1986.
- *Folklore from Contemporary Jamaicans.* Knoxville: University of Tennessee Press, 1985.
- *From My People: 400 Years of African American Folklore.* New York: W. W. Norton Company, 2002.
  "'Go Eena Kumbla': A Comparison of Erna Brodber's *Jane and Louisa Will Soon Come Home* and Toni Cade Bambara's *The Salt Eaters.*" *Caribbean Women Writers: Essays from the First International Conference.* Ed. Selwyn R. Cudjoe. Wellesley: Calaloux, 1990. 169-84.
- *Here Am I: Miscellaneous Meanderings, Meditations, Memoirs, and Melodramas.* Jacksonville, FL: Adducent, 2020.
- *Honey, Hush! An Anthology of African American Women's Humor.* New York: W. W. Norton & Company, 1998.
- "An Interview with Paule Marshall," *Southern Review* 28:1 (1992): 1-20. Reprinted in James C. Hall and Heather Hathaway, *Conversations with Paule Marshall. Jackson*: UP of Mississippi, 2010. 96-115.
- *Land of the Free... Negroes: A Historical Novel.* Jacksonville: Adducent, 2020.
- *The Lineage of Abraham: The Biography of a Free Black Family in Charles City, VA*, With Daryl Lynn Dance, 2022. (Originally published in 1998)
- *Long Gone: The Mecklenburg Six and the Theme of Escape in Black Folklore.* Knoxville: University of Tennessee Press, 1987.
- "*Shuckin' and Jivin*": *Folklore from Contemporary Black Americans.* (Bloomington, Indiana: Indiana University Press, 1978.
- *Till Death Us Did Part: A Story of Four Widows.* Self-published, 2020.

De Veaux, *Alexis. In Celebration of Our Triumph. Conversations with Paule Marshall.* Ed. James C. Hall and Heather Hathaway. Jackson: UP of Mississippi, 40-53 (reprinted from *Essence* 10 (1979).

Gabbin, Joanne Veal. *Shaping Memories: Reflections of African American Women Writers.* Jackson: University Press of Mississippi, 2009.

Hughes, Langston. "'The Negro Artist and the Racial Mountain.'" *The Norton Anthology of African American Literature.* Ed. Henry Louis Gates, Jr., and Nellie Y. McKay. New York: W. W. Norton, 2004. 1311-1314. Reprinted from *The Nation*, June 23, 1926: 692-94. And -- *The Weary Blues.* New York: Alfred A. Knopf, 1926.

Kincaid, Jamaica. *Annie John.* New York: Farrar Straus Giroux, 1983.

By Paule Marshall:

- *Brown Girl, Brownstones: A Novel.* 1959. Old Westbury, New York: The Feminist Press, 1981.
- *The Chosen Place, The Timeless People.* New York: Random House, 1969.

- *Daughters*. New York: Atheneum, 1991.
- *The Fisher King*. New York: Scribner, 2000.
- *Praisesong for the Widow*. New York: G. P. Putnam's Sons, 1983.
- *Reena and Other Stories*. New York: The Feminist Press, 1983.
- *Soul Clap Hands and Sing*. 1961. Washington, D. C.: Howard University Press, 1988.
- *Triangular Road: A Memoir*. New York: BasicCivatis Books, 2009.

Meriwether, Louise. *Fragments of the Ark: A Novel*. New York: Pocket Books, 1994.

ABOUT THE AUTHOR

Daryl Cumber Dance, Professor Emerita, Virginia Commonwealth University and University of Richmond, is the author of the following books:

- *Shuckin' and Jivin': Folklore from Contemporary Black* Americans (Bloomington, Indiana: Indiana University Press, 1978).

- *Folklore from Contemporary Jamaicans* (Knoxville: University of Tennessee Press, 1985).

- *Long Gone: The Mecklenburg Six and the Theme of Escape in Black Folklore* (Knoxville: University of Tennessee Press, 1987).

- *Fifty Caribbean Writers: A Bio-Bibliographical and Critical Sourcebook* (Westport, Connecticut: Greenwood Press, 1986).

- *New World Adams: Conversations with Contemporary West Indian Writers* (Leeds, England: Peepal Tree Books, 1992). Second edition published in 2008.

- *Honey, Hush! An Anthology of African American Women's Humor* (New York: W. W. Norton & Company, 1998).

- *The Lineage of Abraham: The Biography of a Free Black Family in Charles City, VA*, 1999. Self-published. New and expanded edition with Daryl Lynn Dance in 2020.

- *From My People: 400 Years of African American Folklore* (New York: W. W. Norton Company, 2002).

- *In Search of Annie Drew, the Mother, and Muse of Jamaica Kincaid* (Charlottesville: University of Virginia Press, 2016).

- *Till Death Us Did Part: A Story of Four Widows*, 2020.

- *Here Am I: Miscellaneous Meanderings, Meditations, Memoirs, and Melodramas.* Jacksonville, FL: Adducent, 2020.

- *Land of the Free... Negroes: A Historical Novel.* Jacksonville, FL: Adducent, 2020.

Printed in the USA
CPSIA information can be obtained
at www.ICGtesting.com
JSHW070759060324
57837JS00016B/26

9 781962 729000